Macramé

By the Editors of Sunset Books and Sunset Magazine

LANE BOOKS MENLO PARK, CALIFORNIA

FOREWORD

Macramé, the art of knot tying, is a creative and satisfying handcraft that will permit you to find personal expression in your own work of art. Although macramé has been used for centuries for utilitarian and decorative purposes, it has just recently regained its popularity as a handcraft. Macramé's popularity has spread because it is a versatile, inexpensive, and transportable hobby that can be worked on almost any place and any time.

This book was planned for the macramé enthusiast who would like to learn the basic knot techniques and develop his own individual skills. Directions are given for the decorative and practical macramé projects that illustrate some of the unique methods of combining the elementary knots. Because craft stores carry such a wide and ever-changing variety of cords and yarns, we have mentioned general guidelines rather than to recommend specific materials when purchasing cord for a project.

Edited by Susan S. Lampton

Special Consultants: Marion Ferri, Virginia Summit
Layout and Design: Alyson Smith Gonsalves
Illustrations: Susan S. Lampton

PHOTOGRAPHS

FRONT COVER: Macramé handbag with simple weaving by Gerta Wingerd (pages 50 and 67), and square-knotted leather belt by Linda Weingarten (page 30). Photographed by GEORGE SELLAND, MOSS PHOTOGRAPHY. Design consultant: JOHN FLACK.

INSIDE FRONT COVER: All photographs by ALYSON SMITH GONSALVES except "Child's Project, Mr. Seymour Centipede," photographed by MARION FERRI.

INSIDE BACK COVER: All photographs by MARION FERRI except "Waxed Linen Necklace" and "Necklace" (center) photographed by MARK LEWIS.

BACK COVER: Photographed by ALYSON SMITH GONSALVES.

Most of the photographs in this book are by ALYSON SMITH GONSALVES. Exceptions are as follows: EDWARD BIGELOW: 65 (top), 69 (bottom left center). CHARLES BRAY: 52 (bottom right), 53 (bottom left), 57 (top right), 64 (bottom right). ROBERT COX: 43 (top). MARION FERRI: 5 (top), 54 (bottom left), 58 (bottom left), 64 (bottom left), 66 (bottom right), 68 (top right, bottom left and right), 74 (top). ART HUPY: 4 (bottom center and right). SUSAN S. LAMPTON: 10 (top left, bottom left and right), 33 (bottom), 35 (top), 42 (center right), 50 (center right, bottom right), 54 (top), 55 (top right), 57 (bottom left), 70 (top and bottom right), 76 (top), 78 (top left). JACK McDOWELL: 4 (bottom left and detail), 58 (top left, center right, bottom right), 59 (top right), 65 (bottom), 66 (top right). JOYCE NEWCOMB: 69 (top left). WILLIAM C. SEDLACEK: 30 (top right, bottom right and detail), 31 (bottom left and detail), 32 (top right and detail), 34 (top, bottom), 38 (top, bottom), 41 (bottom right and detail), 53 (top right, bottom right), 55 (center left), 57 (bottom center). WILLIAM J. SHELLEY: 28 (bottom right), 35 (center right), 36 (top, bottom), 37 (top, bottom), 57 (bottom right, top and bottom), 58 (top right), 64 (top left), 66 (top left), 68 (top left), 69 (top right). BLAIR STAPP: 42 (top right).

Executive Editor, Sunset Books: David E. Clark

Eighth Printing May 1974
Copyright © Lane Magazine & Book Company, Menlo Park, California.
First Edition. World rights reserved.

Library of Congress No. 75-157172 SBN Title No. 376-04541-8
Lithographed in the United States.

CONTENTS

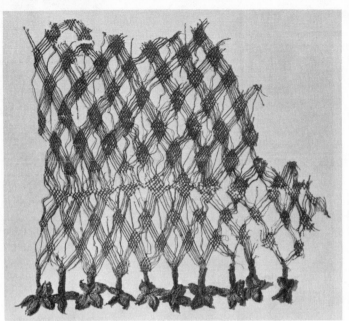

Courtesy Museum of Fine Arts, Boston

*EGYPTIAN NET (above), Indian headdress (right)
are similar although made hundreds of years apart.*

Courtesy of Oakland Museum, Oakland, California

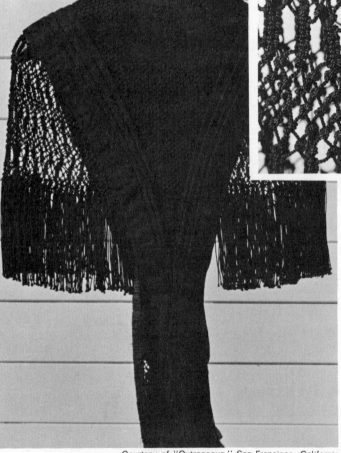

Courtesy of "Outrageous," San Francisco, California

*VICTORIAN JACKET with macramé sleeves shows
concern for precise detail in this era.*

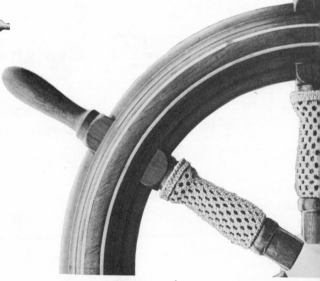

*THE SAILOR'S MACRAMÉ adorned
many parts of his ship.*

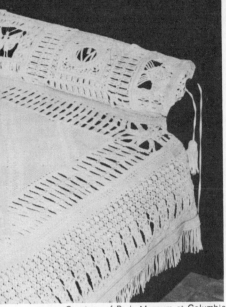

Courtesy of Park Museum at Columbia

MACRAMÉ bedspread, circa 1880's.

INTRODUCING MACRAMÉ

Macramé, pronounced mak-ré-ma, comes from either a nineteenth-century Arabic term, "miqramah," which meant veil, or from the Turkish word for towel, "maqramah." Both the veil and towel were adorned with a knotted fringe. This handcraft probably developed when man first needed to attach two lengths of cord into a single piece or bind two objects together. The square and hitch knots most likely date back to paleolithic or neolithic man. These primitive people undoubtedly used these knots in their daily lives. As time passed, knots were used for a variety of utilitarian, mnemonic, and superstitious purposes. However, once the beauty of the knots themselves was recognized, a new art form emerged.

Actual examples of knotting date back to early Egyptian culture, where knots were used in fish nets (see photograph, top left) and in decorative fringes. The Incas of Peru used a Quipu which was constructed of mnemonic knots (basically overhand knots). It aided them in recording and conveying information. In classical Greece, knots were used in medicine (as slings for broken bones) and in games (the Gordian knot was one such puzzle). Both the early Egyptians and Greeks used the "Hercules" knot (square knot) which had magical or religious connotations on their clothing, jewelry, and pottery. The sailors on ancient sailing ships sometimes carried a knotted cord which legend claimed witches had tied. The knotted cord supposedly bound the winds and therefore controlled the destiny of the sailing ship.

Knotting techniques were probably spread far and wide by sailors, who in their leisure hours would create multitudes of knotted items to decorate the ships (see photograph, bottom right), to trade, or to give as gifts. Macramé in a sailor's vocabulary was better known as "McNamara's Lace," or "square knotting," because the square knot predominated their work. Evidence of macramé reaching North America can be seen in the work of the Northern California Indians after contact with the Europeans (see headdress shown at top right). In the Victorian era, European society used macramé knots to adorn the stylish gowns and cloaks of the gentry class (see photograph, bottom left). Some craftsmen of this era had even greater ambitions and created larger pieces such as the bedspread shown above.

Today macramé is enjoying a "twentieth-century renaissance." As people find they have more spare time, men, as well as women, are turning to working with their hands and are creating not only utilitarian but aesthetic pieces. Great pleasure can come from creating masterful textile pieces using only the two macramé knots (the hitch and square knot). The combinations and variations of the two are endless, and they lend themselves to many designs in both two and three dimensions. Each person's style of knotting makes his own work unique.

Macramé is an international art you will find anywhere from Europe to mainland China. It is a craft for all ages and capabilities. The only necessary equipment is the cord for knotting, possibly some pins, and a working surface. Most macramé can be carried with you and worked on inconspicuously at any time.

Once you have learned the basic techniques, your desire to knot is insatiable. If you are the first in your home to attempt macramé, you will soon find your entire family engrossed in the tying of knots.

EQUIPMENT FOR MACRAMÉ

Pictured on the opposite page are some of the most popular pieces of equipment used for macramé. These are only suggestions, for macramé can be enjoyed and accomplished with the minimum amount of equipment. Be inventive and make an effort to discover equipment suited to your own style of working.

Working Surfaces

Often the working surface depends on the size of your project, the material you are using, and where you like to spend your time knotting.

• CEILING TILE is a very popular working surface because it is light, portable, and firm. The greatest disadvantage of this board is that the surface begins to chip away after extended use. Ceiling tile is available at lumber supply stores as well as at certain weaving shops which carry macramé supplies.

• FELT OR PAPER COVERED CEILING TILE does not chip and is a pleasant surface to work on. Attach the felt or paper by folding it completely around the board and staple or pin it onto the back of the board.

• CUSHION, PILLOW, OR BOLSTER is a portable surface. Use pins which are long enough to stay into the cushion and be careful not to use a cushion which is covered with a material that pins will scar.

• A FOAM RUBBER SLAB glued to light plywood board is a sturdy but soft surface. The wood is not necessary, but it keeps the foam from bending. Select a firm piece of foam thick enough so your pins will not go through. Foam rubber can be found at most department stores and upholstery shops and at foam rubber supply stores.

• FOAM RUBBER BED REST cut at an approximate 45° angle is at a perfect slant to be placed on a table for knotting or rested on your knees. Long pins work best with this, and a material cover makes a more pleasant surface for knotting.

• A CLIP BOARD is best suited for projects such as belts which do not need extensive pinning. A thin sheet of cork board can be clipped to the clip board to facilitate pinning the macramé in place.

Pins

Nearly every project needs to be secured to a working surface. Pins are the best solution, but, surprisingly, there is a variety to choose from.

• T-PINS come in different sizes. They are sturdy and easy to push into hard surfaces. The disadvantage is the bar on top which often catches the strings while you work. T-pins can be purchased in dime stores, hardware stores, upholstery shops, weaving and yardage shops.

• HAT PINS OR CORSAGE PINS are very long but not as sturdy as the T-pin. They are excellent to use in the soft surfaces; cords do not catch on the head of this pin. They can be found in most dime stores or yardage shops.

• PLASTIC HEADED SEWING PINS are very small. Because they come in large quantities, they are good for projects calling for extensive pinning. They can be purchased in any dime store or yardage shop.

Extras

Miscellaneous items are those pieces which might enhance your macramé project or which might be used for fastenings or for finishing touches. Also shown are two items used to keep cord ends neat while you work your macramé projects.

• PLASTIC BOBBINS, although not pliable and sometimes cumbersome, are a good means of wrapping excessive cord. They can be found in weaving shops or in stores which might carry macramé or lace supplies.

• SMALL RUBBER BANDS are used to secure ends which have been wrapped into "butterfly bobbins" (see page 11). They leave the cord ends loose enough to feed out easily when you need more cord.

• FOUND OBJECTS AND ACCESSORIES are used to enhance your macramé project, add points of interest, or act as a means of fastening or finishing. Some of the easiest objects to find and to incorporate into your macramé are shells, beads, bells, rings, and pieces of driftwood. These decorative accents are best discovered in nature rather than in stores, but bells, drapery rings, belt buckles, etc., can be purchased in novelty shops, dime stores, antique stores, drapery shops, leather shops, and secondhand stores.

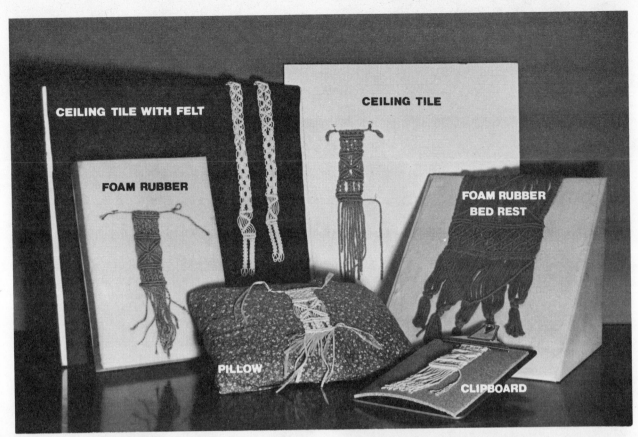

CEILING TILE WITH FELT

FOAM RUBBER

CEILING TILE

FOAM RUBBER BED REST

PILLOW

CLIPBOARD

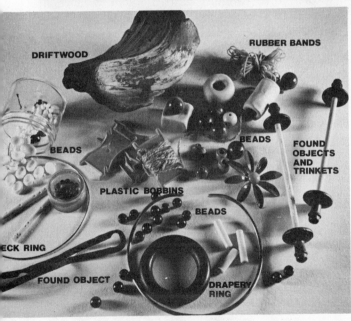

DRIFTWOOD

RUBBER BANDS

BEADS

BEADS

FOUND OBJECTS AND TRINKETS

PLASTIC BOBBINS

BEADS

NECK RING

FOUND OBJECT

DRAPERY RING

VARIOUS PIECES of equipment: working surfaces, pins, and found objects, give a variety of choices to the beginning enthusiast although little or no equipment is essential. Choose items most suitable to your style of knotting.

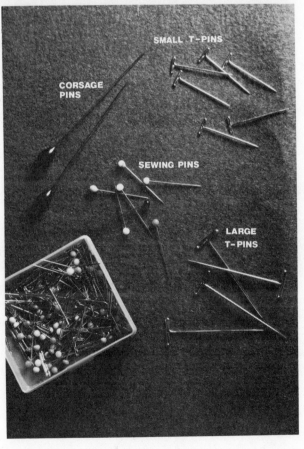

SMALL T-PINS

CORSAGE PINS

SEWING PINS

LARGE T-PINS

Virginia Summit

JUTE is very popular but can shed and fade.

MATERIALS FOR MACRAMÉ

Any material that can be purchased in great lengths and that is pliable can be used for macramé. Possible materials for a macramé project range from kite string or sisal rope to surgical tubing or fine wire. The greatest concerns are to find a material which can be knotted easily but is not too stretchy; one which will lend itself well to the knots you use; and one which will enhance the design as well as the individual knots. The yarns and cords can be broken down into three general groups: yarns derived from plants, animals, man (synthetics).

In the plant category are the more popular yarns —jute, linen, and cotton. These three are the most pleasurable to work with because they knot well, come in a variety of weights, can be dyed, and are readily available. Some of the yarns come with a finish on them such as wax, creosote, or sizing. They can, however, be purchased in their basic form. Jute is a fine material for macramé, but it will fade if constantly exposed to the sun, and it has a tendency to shed during the knotting (see sampler, above). Linen is a beautiful material to work with, but it costs much more than the other two (see sampler, top right). Cotton can be found in many forms, from stiff polished cotton to soft rug yarn which is sometimes combined with a synthetic fiber (see sampler at right).

Animal yarns include the wools and various imported yarns such as mohair, alpaca, etc. These yarns normally have the greatest color range, but they also have a tendency to stretch and break under less tension than the yarns from plants (see sampler, at right).

Man-made or synthetic fibers include nylon, rayon, and orlon to mention only a few. Nylon has a silk-like quality to it (see sampler, bottom right). As it does unravel easily, it is necessary to melt the ends with a wood-burning tool (to prevent blackening) or with a flame. Another method is to dip the ends in clear nail polish. It can be purchased in widths ranging from fishing line to rope diameters. Nylon, however, is very slippery to work with and does not hold knots well. The synthetics are sometimes combined with natural fibers such as cotton or wool. This combination gives the fiber a little more elasticity; the synthetics by themselves do not have this quality.

Other fibers and knotting materials may not be as easy to locate. Silks, though beautiful and strong, are expensive. Leather strips are excellent as knotting material but are usually available in only one length. You can buy a piece of leather and cut the strips by first drawing an accurate spiral on the leather, then carefully cutting it out with small scissors or a small blade. Raffia is a flat, unpliable straw which is interesting to work with but does not show the detail of the individual knots (see sampler on pillow, page 7).

Many of the materials discussed here can be purchased in dime stores, hardware stores, weaving and yarn shops, grocery stores, upholstery shops, leather stores, marine supply stores, or from craft suppliers and cordage companies. When you select your material, choose one which is strong enough to be knotted and one which is long enough for your project (see page 11 for determining lengths).

Virginia Summit

WOOL (left) has greatest color range. Linen (below) is elegant but expensive.

Virginia Summit

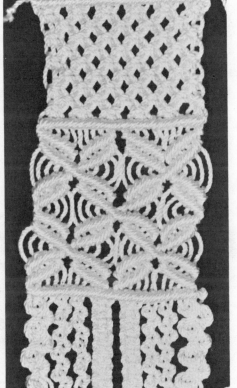

Kathryn Arthurs

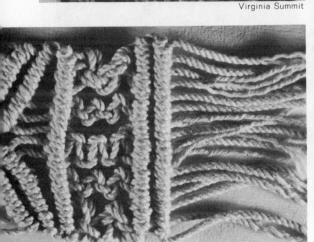

Virginia Summit

COTTON SEINE TWINE (left) and nylon (above) are found in all-purpose stores.

TWO BASIC KNOTS, hitch and square knot (at left, top and bottom) lend themselves to innumerable variations such as a simple chain. (A square-knot chain is shown above.)

ALL AGES ENJOY tying macramé knots and time passes quickly when learning basic techniques and variations.

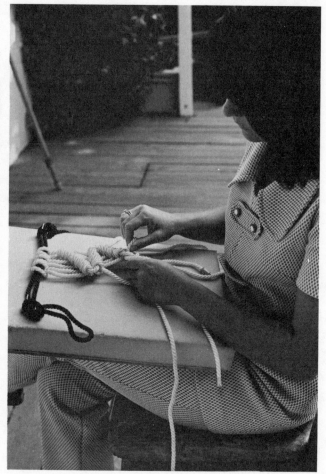

LEARNING THE BASIC KNOTS

Every craft requires some instruction before you begin making finished projects. However, it is a pleasant surprise to discover that in macramé there are only two knots to learn, and one of them you probably accomplished in your scouting days. The real challenge comes when you try to discover new ways of combining the knots or using them in a way no one else has.

• USING THE INSTRUCTIONS. Learn the knots completely and approach them one by one in the order given here. The chapter starts with the overhand knot and illustrates some of the many variations of this one knot. The step-by-step photographs show white, gray, and black cords, so if you use the same tones, the instructions will be extremely easy to follow. Cut the cords long enough to do each exercise. In some instances, the cords for one knot can be used for another series of knots. But most knots have been purposely isolated so that you can concentrate on one element at a time.

In almost every instance, the black cord represents the holding cord or the mounting cord. The gray or white cords are the tying cords. The finished knots in each exercise have been knotted loosely for easy viewing. As you become adept at macramé, you acquire a style of knotting which is comfortable for you. Two people can knot the same pattern and turn out two radically different pieces. So do not feel you are doing it incorrectly if your knotting does not resemble the sample exactly.

• PREPARING FOR KNOTTING. To determine the cord lengths you will need in your practicing and projects involves simple arithmetic. Determining lengths can never take into account the individual style of knotting, the material you use, or the pattern you choose; therefore, it cannot be calculated to the inch. Generally a good rule is to calculate, then overcalculate. Suggestions for what to do if you do run out of cord are covered on page 56.

You can approximate fairly closely the length of cord needed by deciding first how long you want your piece to be. Each cord should be at least four to five the times the finished length of the project. However, since each cord is usually doubled when it is mounted on the heading piece (such as a buckle or frame), it should be cut eight to ten times the length of the finished project. If the pattern you use is very lacy with few knots, possibly you will only need six to seven times the finished length. Depending on the thickness or thinness of a cord, you will have to make compensations in determining the length. Figure a longer length for thicker cords and a shorter length for very fine cords.

• WRAPPING A BOBBIN. Long pieces of cord have a tendency to tangle. When this is the case, a "butterfly bobbin" is the best method of wrapping up the excessive cord. Starting approximately six to eight inches below the mounting knot, pull the cord between your thumb and first finger. Bring it in front of the first two fingers and behind the last two fingers. Then continue in a figure-eight pattern looping it around two fingers at a time (see illustration). Slip the cord off your hand by holding it in the center of the figure eight. Put a rubber band around the center of the bundle to hold it secure; the bobbin will feed cord as you need it in your knotting.

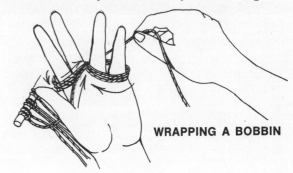

WRAPPING A BOBBIN

THE OVERHAND KNOT

The overhand knot is one of the simplest knots used, although it is not considered a basic macramé knot. It requires only one or more tying cords and no holding cord. An overhand knot can be used in fringes, in chains, or any-place you need a secure or finishing knot.

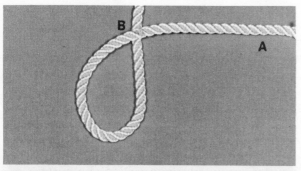

1. Cut a twelve-inch cord to practice this knot. Make a loop with the cord by placing end A over end B.

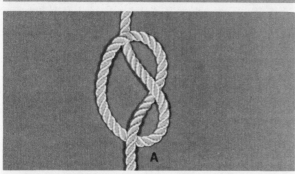

2. Bring end A behind and out through the loop.

3. Pull knot tight or leave it loose. Knot several in a row to create a chain.

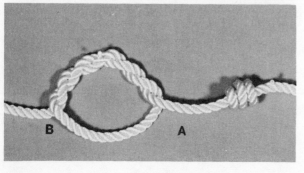

4. A simple and very effective variation is to bring end A around and through the loop several times, then pull the two ends until a barrel-like knot is formed (see photograph to the left).

MOUNTING THE CORDS

The mounting knot is used to secure the cords onto a support from which you will begin your macramé piece. The knot can be done two ways. Both are demonstrated in the following photographs.

Cut several white cords each approximately ten inches long. Cut a black cord ten inches long or use a dowel or other firm object around which you can mount the cords. Knot an overhand knot at each end of the black cord, then pin it across your working surface sticking the pins through the two knots.

Mounting Knot with Bar in Back

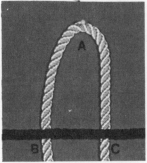 

1. Fold the white cord in half. Place loop A under the black holding cord.
2. Bring loop A down and in front of the holding cord.

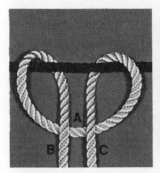 

3. Pull ends B and C down through loop A.
4. Pull the knot tight and repeat the process with the remaining cords. The loop should be in back instead of in front.

Mounting Knot with Bar in Front

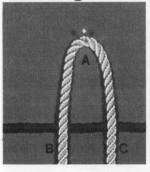 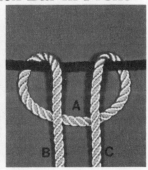

1. Fold one of the white cords in half. Place loop A over the black holding cord.
2. Pull loop A down behind the black holding cord and behind ends B and C.

3. Pull ends B and C down through loop A.
4. Pull knot tight. Compare this knot to the other mounting knot. The loop should be in front instead of in back.

THE HALF-HITCH KNOT

The half hitch is the first step in the double half hitch, which is one of the two basic knots used in macramé. It consists of one holding cord and one tying cord. Because it is simply a single loop, the half hitch is rarely used by itself.

1. Cut a black holding cord approximately eight inches long. Pin one knotted end (overhand) of the black holding cord securely to the working surface. Take a white cord approximately twelve inches long and place it under the black cord with six inches of the white cord above and six inches below. Hold the loose end of the black cord horizontally in one hand and with the other hand bring end B up over the holding cord.

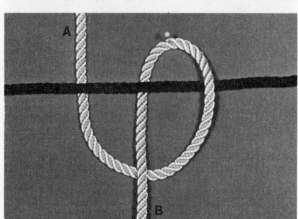

2. Pull end B back down behind the black holding cord and out through the loop which is formed.

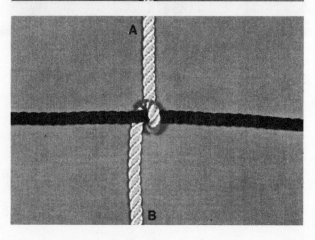

3. Pull end B as tightly as possible. Take two or three more white tying cords and repeat the process on the same holding cord. Notice how loose all the knots are.

THE DOUBLE HALF HITCH

The double half hitch is just two half hitches knotted in succession using the same tying cord. It is a secure knot and has a variety of uses.

1. Pin a black holding cord (approximately eight inches long) to the working surface. Repeat steps for a single half hitch. Then take end B back up over the black holding cord.

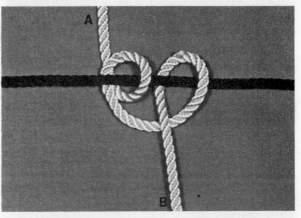

2. Pull end B down behind the holding cord and out through the loop formed by the two half hitches.

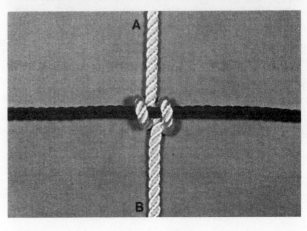

3. Pull loop tight. With only an extra loop, notice how the knot becomes very secure.

LINES OF DOUBLE HALF HITCHES

By varying the placement of the holding cord, it is possible to create designs using several double half hitches tied in succession. Cut a mounting cord ten inches long and four tying cords twenty inches long.

• STRAIGHT BAR. Mount the four cords onto the mounting cord, then pin a ten-inch holding cord at one end; hold it over the tying cords and parallel to the mounting cord. Knot a double half hitch with each cord end over the holding cord. Always keep the holding cord taut.

If a bar, when completed, is not exactly where you want it, it can easily be "erased" by pulling on the holding cord at the beginning of the bar. Since the double half hitches are simply loops around it, the holding cord should slip out easily if you have tied the knots correctly.

• DIAGONAL BAR. An outside tying cord can also be a holding cord. To create a diagonal bar, pin the outside tying cord just under the mounting knot and pull the cord taut at a 45° angle across all the other cords. Tie double half hitches over this diagonal holding cord.

• FREEFORM LINE. To create a freeform line, pull an outside tying cord (holding cord) across the other tying cords but constantly vary the direction of your holding cord while you tie the double half hitches.

Patterns are made by combining double half-hitch bars in a variety of ways. Shown here are the diamond and the daisy—two basic patterns from which additional designs can be created.

DOUBLE HALF-HITCH PATTERNS

The Diamond

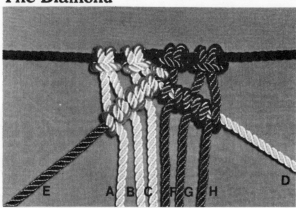

1. Mount four or more cords (each about twenty-four inches long) on a mounting cord which is secured to a working surface. Make half of them white and half of them gray. Take the middle two cords (D and E) and cross them over each other and then over the other cords at an angle. Knot double half hitches on gray holding cord E with the white tying cords. Knot double half hitches on the white holding cord D with the gray tying cords. Always keep the holding cord taut.

2. Tie an overhand knot at the end of these two diagonal rows. Pull white holding cord D at an angle (toward the center) and across the gray tying cords to form a third edge of the diamond. Knot double half hitches on the white holding cord. Pull gray holding cord E over the other white cords and knot double half hitches on it. Once you reach the right holding cord, use it as a tying cord on the gray holding cord.

The Empty Diamond

The empty diamond requires basically the same method of knotting as the regular diamond does, but the center has no cords in it.

1. Start by crossing the two cords in the center as you did with the regular diamond. Knot one double half hitch, but, instead of putting the tying cord aside, hold it with the holding cord. Knot a second double half hitch over both of these cords, then hold this tying cord next to the other two holding cords. This becomes an accumulative edge, growing thicker with each additional holding cord. Continue this process until you complete both sides of the diamond.

CONTINUED ON NEXT PAGE

2. Pull all the cords into an angle to form the bottom half of the diamond. Knot a double half hitch with the last tying cord of the above angle over all the other cords, then put it aside. Take another holding cord and knot another double half hitch over the remaining cords. Continue this on both sides until you have only·two holding cords, one on each side. Use one of the holding cords as a tying cord and knot them together, just as you did in the regular diamond.

The Daisy

Formed by four "petal-like" shapes, the daisy can be used as a flower, or the petals can be used to create an overall pattern (see project, page 35).

1. Mount four tying cords (each about thirty inches long) on a holding cord secured to a working surface. Make half the tying cords white and half gray. Divide them into two equal groups. With outside cord from each side, tie a diagonal row of double half hitches to center to form "V" shape.

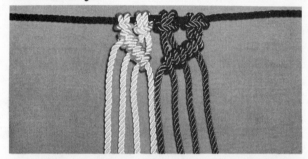

2. Take the next outside cord from each side and knot another diagonal row of double half hitches. Knot the second row somewhat near to, but not flush with the first. Cross the gray and white holding cords of the lower rows either with a double half hitch or a bead.

3. Knot two diagonal rows away from the center, using the white cord as a holding cord on the right and the gray cord as the holding cord on the left.

4. Take the middle two tying cords: pull the white tying cord across the other white tying cords and pull the gray tying cord across the other gray tying cords. Use these two tying cords as holding cords, knot a diagonal row of double half hitches on each side. To achieve the petal effect, gently work the two rows apart with your fingers to make a slight curve. See project on page 35 for completed daisy.

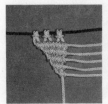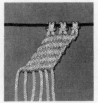

There are ways to shape macramé so you can go beyond the two-dimensional plane and beyond parallel borders. Shown here are two methods.

1. Mount three cords (each about forty inches long) on a mounting cord. Knot one row of double half hitches using the outside cord on the left for a holding cord. Once a row of double half hitches has been knotted, place the holding cord aside and pick up the next outside cord on the left. Pull this across remaining tying cords.

2. Knot a second row of double half hitches and lay this second holding cord aside. Notice that each row is one knot shorter than the row above.

3. Knot remaining rows as you have the first two, until you come to the last row, then knot a single double half hitch.

4. Turn piece so the tip of the triangle is to one side, and the loose cords are all hanging parallel to the mounting cord. Pull the cord which made the last double half hitch across cord ends and perpendicular to the rows of double half hitches. Repeat knotting procedure as before. If you continue making these triangles, eventually a three-dimensional spiral formation will occur (see project, page 36).

1. Using somewhat the same method of knotting as the shaping above, a "stair-stepping" shape can be formed. Mount the same number of cords the same length as before. Pull the left outside cord (holding cord) across and on top of the tying cords, and knot a row of double half hitches. At the end of the row, place the holding cord down next to the tying cords. Using the outside cord on the left, knot a second row. The last knot of this row will be tied with the holding cord of the previous row. Each row will have the same number of knots.

2. Continue knotting rows always using the previous holding cord as a tying cord in the next row.

SHAPING WITH DOUBLE HALF HITCHES

Shaping Number One

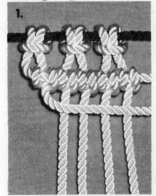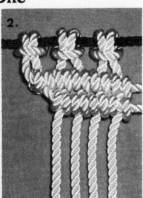

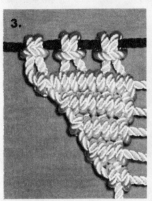

Shaping Number Two

HALF-HITCH CHAINS

Chains are created by using the same tying cords to produce a succession of knots on the same vertical holding cords. A few variations are shown here.

Half and Double Half-Hitch Chains

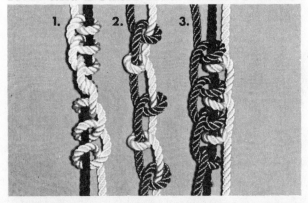

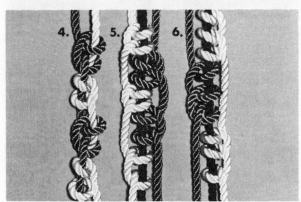

Reverse Double Half-Hitch Chain

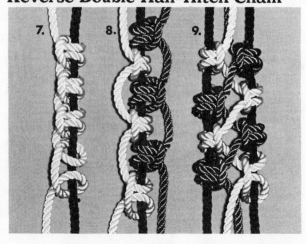

The half-hitch chain is worked with one or more tying and holding cords. The knots, tied vertically in succession, produce a natural twist.

Pin a holding cord and a tying cord vertically to a working surface (example 1). Put the tying cord over the holding cord, around behind it, and out through the loop. As the knots twist, your tying cord will end up on the opposite side of the holding cord from which you started. At this point, pull the tying cord around and behind the holding cord to its original position and continue knotting.

Two variations, the alternate half-hitch and alternate double half-hitch chain (examples 2 and 4), can be worked with two tying cords. Each cord alternates from tying to holding cord as shown at the left.

For two other chain variations, use a holding cord with the alternate half hitches and alternate double half hitches (examples 3 and 5).

A third variation (example 6) carries the previous chain one step further by adding one half hitch to each double half hitch. Three loops are formed with each tying cord.

The reverse double half hitch is accomplished by first pulling the tying cord over, around, and behind the holding cord; then bringing the tying cord over the tying end and parallel to the holding cord. Next pull tying cord under, around, and on top of the holding cord and through the loop. Example 7 shows this reverse double half hitch tied consecutively. Example 8 alternates the knots with two tying cords on a single holding cord creating loops between each knot (see belt, page 32). In example 9, the two outside cords are holding cords. Cross the two middle tying cords and tie reverse double half hitches on the outside holding cords; repeat the process. Notice that the cord from the right knot is always placed on top when the two tying cords are crossed.

VERTICAL DOUBLE HALF HITCH

The vertical double half hitch is a good knot to use for variation in a large section of double half-hitch bars. The terms are just reversed from those in the double half hitch: the holding cord becomes the single tying cord, and all the tying cords become holding cords.

When determining the lengths of your cord in projects with vertical double half hitches, allow for the rapid depletion of the one tying cord.

1. Mount three cords, each approximately sixteen inches long, for the vertical "holding cords." Cut one "tying cord" approximately thirty inches long and pin it (A) to the left side of the holding cords. Bring end A under first holding cord B, then down over, around, and behind B.

2. Repeat, bringing end A down, over, around, and behind holding cord B. Then pull A out through the loop formed. This creates the vertical double half hitch.

3. Pull knot tight and continue knotting vertical double half hitches on each holding cord. Remember to always begin with the horizontal tying cord under the vertical holding cord.

4. To make a second row, use the same tying cord A pulled back towards the left. Pull end G on top of tying cord A. Pull A down over, around, behind, and through the loop formed. Then continue, bringing A down, over, around, behind, and through the loop.

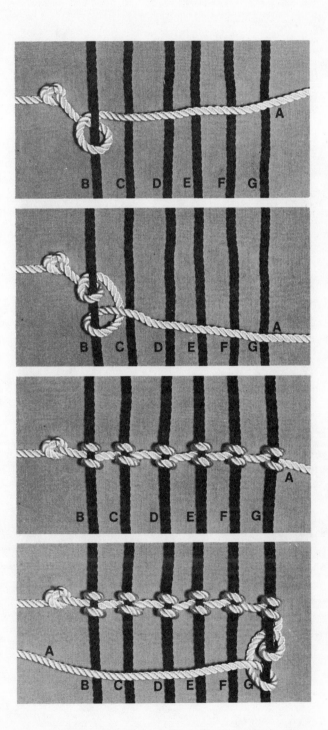

THE HALF KNOT

The half knot is the first part of a square knot. Like the half hitch, the half knot is rarely used by itself; but when it is knotted vertically in a series, it creates a lovely twisting chain.

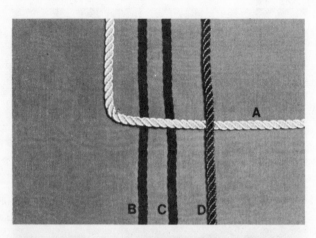

1. Cut four cords (one white, one gray, and two black) approximately ten inches long. Pin them in the order shown in the photograph. The white and gray are tying cords; the two black cords are holding cords. (If you would like to mount the cords, cut two cords about thirty-six inches long and fold them in half, then mount them onto a mounting cord.)

Pull white tying cord A across both black holding cords B and C and under tying cord D.

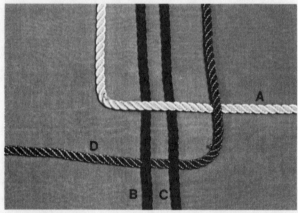

2. Bring gray tying cord D under holding cords B and C.

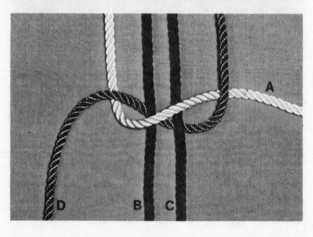

3. Bring gray cord D up through the loop formed between holding cord B and tying cord A. Pull the two tying cords A and D gently to tighten them.

THE HALF-KNOT CHAIN

The half-knot chain is made from half knots repeated vertically. Like the half-hitch chain, this one also has a natural twist. If the knot is started with a left tying cord, a twist to the right will result. If the knots are started on the right, the chain will twist to the left.

1. Make a half knot. Then bring left-side gray cord D over two holding cords B and C and under white tying cord A.

2. Bring white tying cord A back under the two holding cords B and C. Pull tying cord A up through loop formed between cords D and B. Pull knot up secure to the first knot. Continue these same steps, always bringing the left-side tying cord over first on top of the holding cords and then under the right tying cord. A twist will begin to occur. Remember to always begin with the left-side tying cord (or the one nearest to this position) and pull it over on top of the two holding cords.

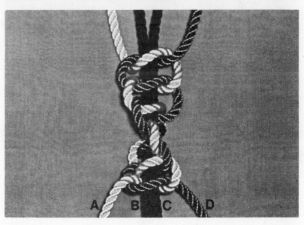

3. As you continue, you will notice it takes a certain number of knots to make a complete twist. This depends on how tightly you are tying and the type of material you are using. Try to be consistent in the number of knots you use in each twist (see project, page 64).

THE SQUARE KNOT

The square knot is the second of the two basic macramé knots. It is most often remembered as the knot you learned in scouts. Variations and patterns can be created by the number of tying and holding cords used or the way you combine the knot with other knots.

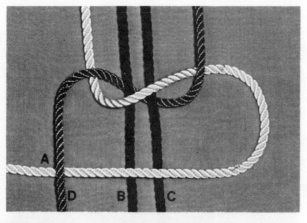

1. Repeat steps one through three of the half knot. Then bring white tying cord A over the two holding cords B and C and under gray tying cord D.

2. Pull gray tying cord D under the two holding cords B and C.

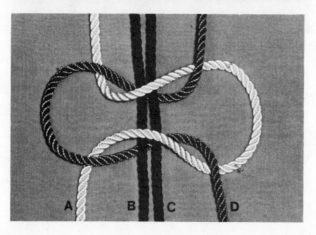

3. Bring gray tying cord D up and out through the loop between A and C.

4. Pull knot tight. Notice how the bar (loop of the gray tying cord) lies on the left of the knot. If you want it to lie on the right, reverse the steps by starting with the right gray tying cord D.

Chains can have as many holding cords as you like, or they can have no holding cords whatsoever. They can also have more than two tying cords.

SQUARE-KNOT CHAINS

1. To make a plain square-knot chain, knot several square knots in succession vertically. Make sure you never bring over a tying cord twice in succession from the same side or the half-knot chain will result.

• VARIATIONS. Use several tying cords without a holding cord and knot "right over left and under, left over right and under" (see example 1).

For another variation, knot several square knots using four holding cords and two tying cords. Lay the two outside tying cords aside and pick up the two outside holding cords. Tie several knots with just these four cords. Switch back to the first two tying cords and tie several square knots with these cords. Alternate this pattern every few knots.

SQUARE-KNOT BOBBLE

An attractive three-dimensional addition to any macramé piece, the bobble is merely a square-knot chain which has been pulled back around itself to form a ball or bobble (see purse on cover).

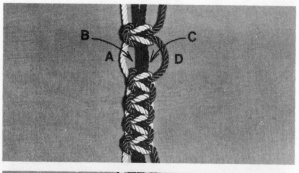

1. Pin four cords (white, two black, and a gray) to a working surface. Cut them long enough to make a small chain. Knot one square knot. Leave some slack, then knot a chain of at least three square knots.

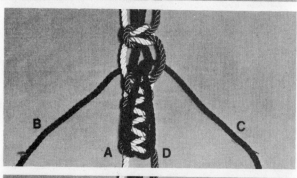

2. Take the ends of holding cords B and C, thread them between B and C in the space between the first and second square knots.

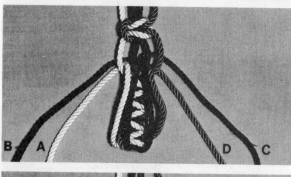

3. Pull white tying cord A up and thread it between white tying cord A and holding cord B. Thread gray tying cord D through the space between holding cord C and tying cord D.

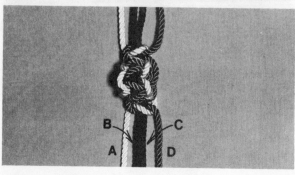

4. Pull all four loose ends down until the chain forms a tight ball. Tie a square knot directly under bobble with tying cords A and D around holding cords B and C. This should secure the bobble in place.

ALTERNATE SQUARE-KNOT PATTERN

The alternate square-knot pattern can be knotted loosely to look very lacy or knotted tightly to achieve a woven like texture (see project, page 34 for one example).

1. Cut six black holding cords and six tying cords (three gray and three white if you want them keyed to the photograph). Have them all about twenty-four inches long. Pin them to a working surface in the order shown in the photograph—one white, two black, one gray, etc. Divide cords into three groups of four. Each group has two tying cords and two holding cords. Starting with either left or right, knot a square knot with each group of four cords.

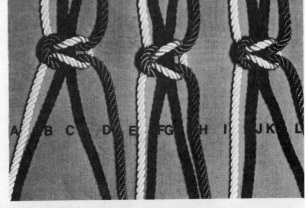

2. Pull the two outside tying cords (A and L) and the two outside holding cords (B and K) aside. Divide the remaining eight cords into two groups of four cords. Tie a square knot with each group. Notice that tying cords D, E, H, and I all become holding cords.

3. Bring the first two and last two cords (A, B, and K, L) down and knot a third row of three square knots using the same cords and same knotting order as row one. Alternating from a row of three knots to two knots creates an alternate square-knot pattern.

Martha Heinrichs

Martha Tollette

CANDLE SLING (at top and page 31), neckpiece (above and page 41), and bell pull (at right and page 36) are just three of the many decorative macramé projects you can make.

Sandi Cummings

Gerta Wingerd

TRIM for clothing, see page 32.

PROJECTS FOR THE BEGINNER

Once you have mastered the basic macramé knots, you can apply your new knowledge to actually making finished pieces. The following macramé projects, ranging from practical to decorative, are geared to the beginning enthusiast. Brief instructions explain how to make each item; however, because of the many knot variations and many kinds of materials available, the real planning and designing must come from you. In some instances, two variations of a project are shown with a short explanation of each. Therefore the ideas can serve as inspiration rather than as patterns. For example, the macramé draperies (page 39) could be easily adapted to a wall hanging; the slings for the candles (page 31) could be holders for outdoor plants; the table runners (page 35) could be rugs as well.

Included with each project idea are suggestions as to the type of material to use. You will probably discover favorite materials which will work better in your particular style of knotting. (See page 8 for explanation of material.)

• HOW MUCH MATERIAL DO YOU BUY? In determining how much material to buy, decide on the size (length) of your piece, then multiply this measurement by eight or even ten. Once the cords are mounted (doubled), the working length of the cord will be from four to five times your finished length (this is discussed more fully on page 11). Some projects do not require mounting, such as the sweater trim on page 32 and the shawl on page 34. The cords for these projects need only to be four to five times the finished length.

• MAKING A SAMPLER. A sampler is a more reliable way of determining the length of cords you will need for a particular project. Cut the cords for the sampler at a measured, but arbitrary length and then knot them using the main knots and patterns

you have chosen. Once you reach the ends of your cords, measure the length of the knotted piece. Divide this measurement into the measured length of the cords before knotting. This will give you the number of times you should multiply the desired length of your real project. For example, if your sampler was started with cords thirty inches long, and after they were completely knotted they measured ten inches, you would know that the length of your cords for the real project should be three times longer than the measurement of the finished length.

• ADDING ACCESSORIES. Some projects may require the addition of beads. The beads can be knotted directly into the macramé piece, or they can be attached later by sewing, tying, or gluing. When adding beads into a section of square knots or square-knot chains, thread the holding cords through the center of the bead, then continue knotting square knots below the bead. In the double half hitch, the bead is again threaded onto the holding cord.

To make bead threading easier, dip your cord end into melted wax and shape into a point. Once the project is completed, the waxed end can be cut off.

There are ways to enlarge certain bead holes if they are too small for the number of cords you are trying to thread. Wooden beads can be held in a vise, and the hole drilled larger. The hole in a plastic bead can be enlarged by using a metal knitting needle which has a greater circumference than the hole. Heat the needle, then push it through the hole. This melts the plastic and enlarges the hole. Ceramic and glass beads are delicate and do not lend themselves to drilling. If it is impossible to get a cord through the hole of these beads, thread a smaller cord through the hole, then tie the bead in place.

LEATHER BELT OF SQUARE KNOTS

This leather belt, made completely in the alternate square-knot pattern, can be of any material as long as it is durable and not too bulky. Leather strips can be found uncut and in varying widths in leather shops, shoe repair stores, and some crafts stores. If you cannot locate the uncut leather strips, purchase a piece of thin leather. Draw a spiral on it and cut the spiral out with scissors or a knife. This will make a continuous strip of leather.

Measure four strips at least eight times the finished length, then mount them onto two rings held together. Tie one square knot below the rings with center four cords. For the second row, tie two square knots with the outer four cords on either side (see page 27, alternate square-knot pattern). Continue the pattern to the desired length; cut the cord ends into an even fringe.

Linda Weingarten

LEATHER BELT was mounted on brass rings and tied in alternate square-knot pattern.

VERTICAL DOUBLE HALF-HITCH BELT

The finishing touch to this belt is the buckle made by gluing the loose ends of the cords between two strips of leather. As the vertical double half-hitch knot rapidly depletes the length of cord used as a tying cord, cut an unusually long tying cord, more than the regular four to five times the desired length.

Determine the width you would like the belt, then mount the number of cords on three separate buckles as shown in the illustration. (These cords need not be much longer than the finished length of the belt.) Cut a separate tying cord and pin it to the board perpendicular and across the holding cords. (Remember—always bring the one tying cord under the holding cord when you start a knot.)

Knot vertical double half hitches with the cords of the first buckle, then thread a bead on the tying cord and knot a second group of vertical double half hitches (see illustration). Add a second bead and knot a third group of vertical double half hitches. Add beads every few rows.

When you reach the desired length, trim loose ends and glue them between two strips of leather cut to form the end of the buckle.

You can add a small knotted section of double half-hitch bars to hold the leather straps in place when the belt is buckled. Sew the ends of this piece to the wrong side of the belt.

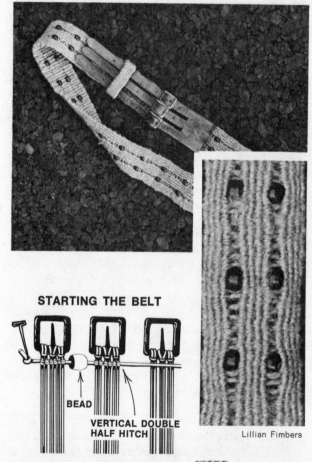

STARTING THE BELT

BEAD

VERTICAL DOUBLE HALF HITCH

Lillian Fimbers

TIGHTLY KNOTTED vertical double half hitches give this belt a woven-like appearance.

CANDLES HANG IN MACRAMÉ SLING

Hanging candles make an attractive decoration and bring interest to an undecorated corner of a room or patio. Place the candle and sling anyplace where subtle light is appealing.

Be sure that the cord you use is strong enough to hold the weight of the candle and is fireproof (use a commercial fire retardant available in most hardware stores), and be sure that the candle is wide enough to keep the flame away from the cord. Another precaution is to keep the wick of the candle clipped short.

A candle sling can be made of any macramé chain. The two shown here were made entirely of square knots. The sling shown at the bottom left was started with six cords mounted on a small ring. The cords were divided into three groups of four cords each. Two outside cords in each group, used to do the tying, were cut about four times the finished length. The holding cords were cut just a bit longer than the finished length. The cords were then knotted into three square-knot chains. The chains were brought together under the candle by tying an overhand knot; and all the cord ends were left as fringe and decorated with contrasting wooden beads.

The sling shown at the bottom right differs from the one shown at left—it is not as long, is knotted with more cords, and uses several variations of the square knot. This sling is worked from bottom to top. Twelve cords were mounted on a small ring which was centered on the bottom of the candle. The cords were divided into three groups of eight cords, and then were knotted in the alternate square-knot pattern. The cords in the three groups were then divided in half, and each half (four cords) was knotted into a short section of twisting half-knot chains. The half-knot chains were then knotted into straight square-knot chains. The half-knot and square-knot chains were repeated up to the top using all the eight cords in each of the three groups. The ends were tied and then glued around the supporting ring. A length of braided cord can be added to this ring for extra length.

SLING in alternate square-knot pattern with square-knot chains decorates yet supports candle well.

Joy Coschigano

SQUARE-KNOT CHAINS make sturdy sling for hanging object. (Also see inside front cover.)

Martha Heinrichs

MACRAMÉ TRIM FOR CLOTHING

A macramé trim can accent a sweater or a piece of clothing, or it can be the finishing touch to a new outfit. Two examples are shown here: one for a sweater, the other for a dressy tunic. Trim is often knotted much like macramé belts—in one long piece with a repetitive pattern; but, border trims do not have to be finished at the ends. Sewing the trim onto the clothing conceals the ends and makes it more a part of the article.

The pattern for the sweater border (see photograph at right) was created by using contrasting colors and diagonal bars of double half hitches. Sixteen cords of very fine yarn were pinned (unmounted) to a board with two cords of contrasting colors on either side of twelve cords of lighter colors. (To determine the length of cords you will need, decide on a finished length and multiply the measurement by four or five.) The cords were wound into bobbins to prevent tangling. Starting a few inches below the pins, the cords were divided into two equal groups. The two middle cords were crossed over one another and held at a diagonal across the remaining cords.

The knotting procedure was the same as for shaping (see page 19), only the holding cords were always held at a diagonal. The knotting was worked on one half of the diamond shape at a time. After the last row of one double half hitch was knotted, the cord which was the first holding cord was pulled down perpendicular to the ends of all the rows of double half hitches. One row of double half hitches was knotted on this holding cord using all the remaining holding cords as tying cords (see illustration). The same procedure was repeated for the second side of the diamond. Each diamond below this was always begun by crossing over the two central cords. Once the desired length was reached, the trim was sewn to the sweater.

The tunic trim (shown at the right) was designed more as a decorative element and as the focal point of the outfit rather than as a repetitive border design. This adornment was created from several macramé chains and patterns which were attached to the tunic in the shapes desired. The pattern of the trim was repeated in the matching belt. The main design, the double half-hitch oval (a diamond without an overhand knot at the points) was repeated in the medallion around the neck, in the sleeve trim, and in the belt. The main knot used was the alternate double half-hitch chain knotted with small loops (picots) left between each knot (see page 20).

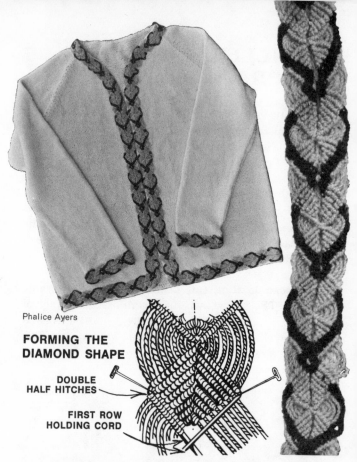

Phalice Ayers

FORMING THE DIAMOND SHAPE

DOUBLE HALF HITCHES

FIRST ROW HOLDING CORD

MACRAMÉ TRIM of fine yarn is an integral part of this hand-knitted sweater.

Gerta Wingerd

TRIM AND MATCHING BELT on this dressy tunic are knotted with "rat-tail" yarn.

A FANCY WATCH BAND

A macramé watch band is attractive, durable, and comfortable. The strap of this watch was begun at the pointed end (the process is described on page 52). It was knotted with twelve cords tied in an alternate square-knot pattern which naturally created holes for the prong of the buckle. Diagonal bars of double half hitches were added for interest, and the watch was tied on with double half hitches over the first bar on the side of the face. The alternate square-knot pattern was continued on the back of the watch face, and double half hitches were knotted onto the second bar on the side. The design

Virginia Summit

MACRAMÉ WATCH BAND in a square-knotted pattern gives your watch a new look and is a quick project.

was knotted to the length desired. The cord ends were looped over the buckle, then sewn to the back side of the strap. A snap can be added to keep the pointed end flush with the strap when it is buckled, or a small chain of square knots can be attached as a band to secure end.

MACRAMÉ FOR MEN—A VEST

Specifically designed for a man, this macramé vest is a simple design. Only the front two panels are knotted—in square knots and vertical and double half hitches. The back is a piece of cloth cut to size and attached to the macramé panels at the sides and shoulder.

The two panels were knotted in separate pieces and started at the bottom. A pattern was cut in the shape desired for the two panels, then pinned to the working surface as a guide. The cords were measured, calculated to fit the bottom width, then mounted. An extra long holding cord was cut because of the vertical double half-hitch sections.

The first panel was started with four rows of double half hitches; then several rows of vertical double half hitches were knotted above this. The "X" pattern was knotted in three sections with bars of double half hitches dividing them. Two bars of double half hitches were knotted above the top group of "X's," then a section of vertical double half hitches was begun at the bottom of the armhole. To make the armhole curve, the cords were eliminated as the knotting proceeded (see illustration). When the knotting was completed, the eliminated ends were trimmed and tacked into the inside of the armhole.

Dr. Charles Stevens

VEST was shaped by eliminating certain cord ends while knotting. (Also see inside front cover.)

VEST PANEL

ELIMINATED CORDS

CHAINS

VERTICAL D.H.H.

DIAMOND

DOUBLE HALF HITCHES

The top part of the vest panel was knotted into sections of square-knot chains divided with double half-hitch bars. Upon completion, all the ends were trimmed and tacked or woven back into the knotting with a needle. The panels were seamed to the back portion at the shoulder and sides.

SHAWL AND MATCHING CAP

Clothing is a challenging project to attempt in macramé. However, a shawl and matching cap made almost entirely in the alternate square-knot pattern are good beginning projects. If a heavy yarn is used, the knotting will go quite fast.

To make the shawl, start in the middle and work out to the ends (see page 51). This allows for a fringe. Begin with thirty-two cords cut approximately five times the desired length. Mark the center of the cords with a rubber band and wrap all the ends into bobbins. Put one half of the cords into a paper bag and pin the other half to a working surface. Knot the alternate square-knot pattern from the center to the end of the first half (see page 27, alternate square-knot pattern). Knot a final row of square knots, then clip the ends to make the fringe. Take the remaining cord ends from the bag and tie alternate square knots directly below the center row. Finish this second half to match the first.

The cap was made from the same material as the shawl. Begin at the crown of the cap by folding all twenty-four cords (cut approximately eight times the desired length) in half and tie an overhand knot at the center point. Knot a circular bar of double half hitches around the overhand knot. Divide the cord ends into groups of four cords each and tie a square knot with each group. At this point, you must add more cords to increase the size of the cap, illustrated below (the gray cords represent the added cords). Knot the alternate square-knot pattern to a point where the cap almost fits your head. Complete it by tying two rows of double half hitches, a row of overhand knots (six cords in each knot), and a final row of double half hitches. Cut all the ends, then sew them into the inside of the cap.

Wilma Long

SIMPLE PATTERNED shawl and cap are warm accessories if knotted with heavy yarn.

ADDING CORDS TO INCREASE SIZE

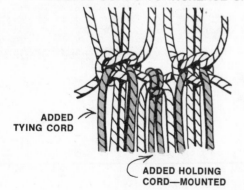

ADDED TYING CORD

ADDED HOLDING CORD—MOUNTED

CAP CAN BE ENLARGED to fit around head by adding cords in the square knot pattern.

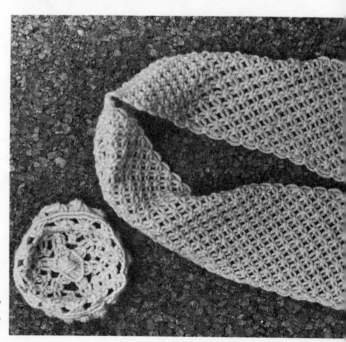

KNOTTED TABLE RUNNER

A macramé table runner can be a lovely decorative element in any table setting and is a good piece on which to practice a variety of knots. When designing your table runner, consider the accessories and china which you will use with it. Choose a yarn which can be cleaned easily; then measure and cut cords four to five times the desired length.

The table runner shown at top right was designed so it could be one continuous piece or ten individual place mats. Each rectangle of the ten sections was bordered by a row of double half hitches. The borders were separated by unknotted cords with four evenly spaced Josephine knots (see page 45). The table runner can be divided into place mats by cutting through the unknotted cords and through the four Josephine knots which will leave a fringe on two sides.

Five different designs were used in the ten place mats: the double half-hitch daisy (page 18), the single petal (page 38), diagonal bars (page 32), the small diamond pattern (page 17), and three large diamonds (middle two place mats) with square knot centers. The piece can be started from either end on a mounting cord, or it can be started in the center. To begin in the middle, the center of the cords was marked with a rubber band. One half of the cords was put into a paper bag, and the other half was pinned to the working surface (see page 51). The knotting was begun below the center point. After one half of the table runner was completed, the other half was taken from the bag. Starting at the center point, the design was knotted to match the first half of the table runner.

The second example, shown at bottom right, was knotted in a more open pattern. This table runner was started at one end with all the cords pinned securely to the board. The two center cords were crossed and pinned at a diagonal to form a point. Double half hitches were tied on the two diagonal cords to secure them in this position. The pattern was continued incorporating double half-hitch diamonds, the alternate square-knot pattern, and square-knot chains. The end was knotted into another double half-hitch point by pulling the two outside cords down at a diagonal toward the center as holding cords. The fringe, at both ends, was divided into five equal groups and tied with an overhand knot.

SIMPLICITY OF PATTERN enhances table runner which is used with many objects.

Virginia Summit

MACRAMÉ TABLE RUNNER can also be cut into ten individual place mats (see detail below).

Jeri Howard

ORIENTAL BELL PULLS

The pagoda effect of the bell pulls was achieved by knotting tight rows of double half hitches in decreasing bars. The unique feature of this design is the three-dimensional shape produced by knotting a flat pattern.

Start with at least six cords and mount them onto a small ring. Be very generous with your measure—allow at least ten to twelve times your finished length for each cord. To form the top section of the pull, knot two chains (six cords each) of half knots. Twist the two chains together to form a solid tube-like shape.

Next, to form the main portion of the pull, begin the double half-hitch shaping (see page 19). Pull the left outside cord across the other cords and use it as the first holding cord. Knot a row of double half hitches, then put this holding cord aside. Bring the next outside left cord across the remainder of the tying cords and knot a second row of double half hitches using it as a holding cord. Put this cord aside. Continue knotting rows of double half hitches without ever using the holding cord as a tying cord once it travels across the other tying cords. Each row has one less double half hitch than the row above. Eventually all the rows form a triangular shape. After you complete one "triangle," turn the piece one quarter of a circle so the tip of the triangle, the last double half hitch, is pointing to the left. Pull the cord which was used as the last tying cord perpendicular to all the previously knotted rows of double half hitches. Knot the second triangle in the same manner as the first. Turn the piece again one quarter of a circle and knot a third triangle (see illustration). Four triangles will produce a square.

For a more graceful line, decrease the size of each square by eliminating one cord. To accomplish this, knot one double half hitch in the first row of the tenth triangle. Hold the first tying cord with the original holding cord. Knot about two thirds of this first row using the two holding cords, then cut off the added holding cord and tuck the end into the knotted row. Complete the row of double half hitches with one holding cord. By eliminating one cord in one quarter of each complete square (every fourth triangle), you will eventually finish with only eight of the twelve cords you started with. To complete the bell pull, loop all but the two outside cords through the bell handle and bring the ends back up next to themselves. With the two outside cords, tie a square-knot chain around all the cord ends. This secures the bell to the square-knot chain.

FORMING A SPIRAL SHAPE

TWO HALF-KNOT CHAINS

DOUBLE HALF HITCH

SPIRAL is caused by knotting double half-hitch triangles continuously in one direction. (Also see inside front cover.)

Sandi Cummings

SHAPING NUMBER ONE (page 19) is the process used to create this shape.

SQUARE-KNOTTED HANDBAG

CONTINUOUSLY KNOTTED around a board, this pattern needs to be seamed only at the bottom.

Marion Ferri

A macramé handbag is a useful and versatile accessory in anyone's wardrobe. Any style or size is possible to make, from a beach bag to an evening purse. But whatever size or style you choose, use a yarn that is colorfast, can be washed or dry cleaned, and can withstand great wear.

This particular bag was made entirely of square knots and demonstrates the variation you can get by knotting with four cords as well as eight cords. It was worked as one piece but can be done in two separate pieces and seamed on the sides (methods for shaping bags are described on page 51). A good working surface to use would be a board about the actual width of the bag, so the mounting cord could be pinned around the circumference of the board. The sixty-four cords for this bag were measured at least eight to ten times the finished length, and then mounted on the circular mounting cord so the pattern could be worked continuously around the bag.

First, four rows of alternating square knots were tied using four cords in each knot. Then three rows of alternating square knots were knotted with eight cords in each knot using the two cords on each side of the four holding cords for tying cords. Next, another three rows of alternating four-cord square knots were tied.

The central design was begun by knotting twelve rows of eight alternate square knots with eight cords per knot. The pattern of alternating eight-cord square knots was decreased to a point by knotting seven rows of square knots starting with seven knots in row thirteen, six in row fourteen, five in row fifteen, etc., until one square knot was tied in row nineteen to form the point. The alternating square knots of four cords each was resumed again under the eight-cord square-knot pattern. The bag

was completed with sixteen rows of four-cord square knots, eight rows on each side of the point and eight rows under the last eight-cord square knot.

The purse was finished by taking all the loose ends on both front and back, then tying sixteen overhand knots of eight cords each leaving an even fringe hanging from each knot.

The bag handle was constructed from twelve cords knotted in alternating square knots. The rings were secured between tying and holding cords of the square knots, and the pattern was continued into the center of the rings. When the desired length was reached, the ends of the twelve cords were tied into overhand knots which were pulled through the spaces between the alternating square knots on the bag. The overhand knots were then sewn into the inside of the bag, and the handle was sewn flush to both sides of the bag. For a finishing touch, the bag can be lined.

HANDLE is separate piece of alternate square knots; rings are decorative element.

MACRAMÉ COVERINGS FOR EXISTING PURSES

A macramé covering can give a new look to an existing handbag. In choosing the purse to be covered, use one which can easily conceal the beginning of your knotting. In some cases the purse can be taken apart (as the one on the right was), and the cords secured under a rim. Any pattern can be used, but the more simple the pattern, the more attractive your handbag will be. Mount enough cords to go completely around the bag. Use a number of cords which can be divided into equal groups and then knot directly on the bag.

The pattern on the purse shown on the right repeats one of the petals in the daisy pattern (see page 18) at an angle. The cords were divided into equal groups of at least six cords each. Starting with one of the groups, a diagonal bar of double half hitches was knotted, bringing the right outside cord across the remaining cords. A second diagonal bar was knotted below the first, going the same direction and using the next outside cord on the right. The two bars were separated by gently working them apart with the fingers until they curved into the shape desired. Once the first horizontal row of petals was knotted using all the groups of cords, a second row was begun by first dividing the cords of each petal. Three cords were pulled to the right, and three cords were pulled to the left. Basically it is an alternating pattern, so three cords of one petal plus three cords of the petal next to it form the petal below (see photograph, at right). After the rows of the pattern were knotted to the bottom of the purse, the extra lengths were trimmed and the ends sewn together. A macramé handle was added under the existing handle by tying a solid strip of knots and then tacking the strip onto the sides and bottom of the bag.

The purse on the left was covered with square knots in alternating vertical rows. The cords were mounted on a cord which was hidden under the rim of the purse. They were then divided into groups of fourteen cord ends. A square knot was tied using the two center cords as holding cords and the next two cords on either side as the tying cords. The tying cords were laid aside after knotting one square knot. A second square knot was knotted under the first using the next two cords on either side of the first tying cords. The process was continued until every cord of the group had been tied in a square knot. The pattern was tied with each group of fourteen cords until the first row was completed. All the tying cords on the right side of the vertical

Wilma Long

Phalice Ayers

KNOTTING A COVER for an existing handbag is sometimes easier than knotting one from scratch. (Also see inside front cover.)

SQUARE KNOT PATTERN

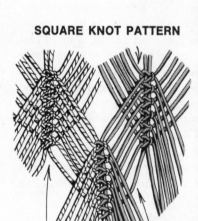

SQUARE KNOT
HOLDING CORD

SQUARE KNOT
TYING CORD

DETAIL PICTURES above show alternating patterns of square-knot chains at left and double half-hitch petals at right.

row of square knots as well as all the tying cords on the left side of another vertical row of knots were then brought together to start the second row (see illustration). The pattern was continued to the bottom of the purse. Notice that all the square knots were knotted the same way, so the bar is always on the same side. The extra ends were knotted together on the bottom of the purse, then trimmed.

DRAPERY, DIVIDER, OR WALL HANGING

These versatile pieces could be used as a window drapery to break up the light without covering the space completely, as a divider to section off portions of a room, or as a wall hanging to decorate an unadorned wall in your home. The biggest challenge here is size. These two examples took little time to make, because the patterns were not complex, and relatively few knots were used. You will need to use a cord which is colorfast and to find a suitable mounting bar. Wooden dowels with ornate knobs for the ends were used for both the draperies shown. The length as well as the width of your cords will depend on the size of the space you plan to cover.

The drapery shown below consists almost entirely of square-knot chains and the alternate square-knot pattern. Over fifty cords were mounted on the dowel; two sizes of cord were used for an interesting effect. Groups of four cords each were knotted into square-knot chains. A large space was left between each knot, and a different number of knots was used in each chain. Between the chains, two cords were left unknotted. The center portion of the drapery (six rows) was knotted entirely in the alternate square-knot pattern. The top pattern was repeated in the bottom half, but each chain has the same number of knots. Then the cords were all tied in the double half hitch to secure them to the bottom dowel. Next the cord ends were divided into equal groups and held together with a separate cord tied in an overhand knot. In the final row, each group was divided, and the halves of adjacent groups were brought together and secured with a separate cord.

The second example, shown below, is smaller but more complicated. Approximately fifty cords were mounted on the dowel, then a second dowel was secured next to the mounting dowel with double half hitches. Square-knot chains were knotted between the four double-edged diamonds. Two more rods were knotted in, and the entire section below them was left unknotted. Two more rods were added, and the middle band was knotted incorporating the alternate square-knot pattern on each side with three double half-hitch "X's" (or daisies) in the center. Side portions of the "X" patterns were knotted in alternate half-hitch chains. The drapery was completed by repeating the top two bands in reverse order. All the ends were tied into double half hitches around two more dowels. The ends were knotted into overhand knots and clipped to the desired length of fringe.

Martha Heinrichs

Jeri Howard

THESE LARGE KNOTTED PIECES can be draperies, wall hangings, or room dividers.

FIGURE-EIGHT BARRETTE

This barrette, a geometric figure-eight design (see illustration), is composed completely of double half hitches. It was made from a medium-weight cord which holds its shape as well as someone's hair.

GEOMETRIC SHAPED BARRETTE

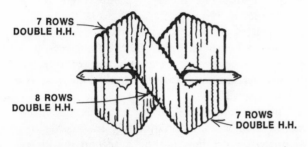

7 ROWS DOUBLE H.H.

8 ROWS DOUBLE H.H.

7 ROWS DOUBLE H.H.

Mount eight cords measured eight times the desired length on a cord. Knot one row of double half hitches, then divide the cords in half with eight ends on the right, eight on the left. Begin the double half-hitch shaping as shown on page 19 with the eight cords on the right. Tie six rows of double half hitches below the top row, always taking the holding cord from the left and pulling it to the right over all the remaining tying cords. Reverse the direction when you reach row seven. Knot eight rows of double half hitches always using the outside right

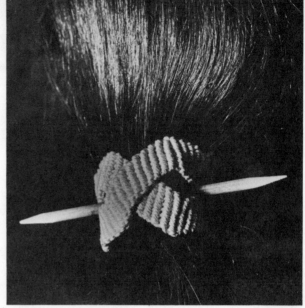

Mary E. Anderson

BARRETTE of medium weight cotton seine twine is washable and durable.

cord as a holding cord. In row fifteen, pull the holding cord from the left to the right and knot six rows of double half hitches.

For the left eight cords, reverse the above instructions. Complete the piece by knotting a final row of double half hitches with all sixteen ends. Trim the cord ends and sew or glue them under. Tack the two ends of the mounting cord under the top row. A pine dowel secures this barrette to the hair.

SIMPLE MACRAMÉ BUTTONS

Macramé buttons, made of a durable material, can be the finishing touch to any outfit. The buttons shown here were made entirely of square-knot chains. Six cords were pinned to the working surface and knotted into a small square-knot chain (four holding cords, two tying cords). All the ends were then pulled back up behind the square knots and threaded out through the space between the two center cords at the top of the chain. The ends were pulled until the bobble formed, then they were divided into two groups of three cords (see illustration). A square-knot chain was knotted with each group (one holding cord, two tying cords). These two chains were pulled tightly around the sides of the bobble, then knotted together at the bottom into a chain with all six cords (see illustration). This last chain was tucked into the back and center of the other chains and glued into place. The button at this point can be sewed directly onto the clothing.

Virginia Summit

FORMING A BUTTON

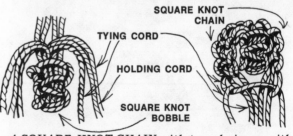

SQUARE KNOT CHAIN

TYING CORD

HOLDING CORD

SQUARE KNOT BOBBLE

A SQUARE-KNOT CHAIN with two chains on either side form elaborate bobble or button.

SQUARE-KNOTTED NECKPIECE

The delicate openwork of this neckpiece is due to the use of the alternate square-knot pattern, the fine cord, and the small beads. It was started on a gold neck ring which hooks in the back. (The ring can be purchased at a jewelry store or at a crafts store carrying jewelry supplies.)

Approximately fifty cords were mounted on the ring. Five rows of the alternate square-knot pattern were tied, then a single row of double half hitches curved to the shape of the ring was knotted. Approximately sixteen cord ends on the left and right side were cut into a fringe. Below the double half-hitch row, the remaining cords in the center were knotted into several small square-knot chains of three square knots each. Then six rows of the alternate square-knot pattern were completed below the chains. Each wooden bead was threaded onto two cords, and the cord ends of about sixteen cords on the left and right side were trimmed into a second fringe. Small square-knot chains were knotted below the beads with just the remaining center cords. Three rows of the alternate square-knot pattern were tied, then eight cords on the left and right side were tied into two square knots separate from the last few rows of the center cords. The ends of these eight outside cords were cut to be shorter than the remainder of the cords which were knotted into four final rows of the alternate square-knot pattern.

Martha Tollette

PROPORTION this neckpiece to your size and height. A fine cord works best.

PENDANT NECKLACE

The major point of interest in this necklace is the small pendant with the wooden beads. Simple in design, this piece would complement any outfit. The necklace was started in the center of the pendant just below the beads where twelve cords were mounted onto a long cord. The cord ends were divided into six groups of four cords. Each group was tied into a square-knot chain about one inch long. The two outside chains were then pulled up to form two sides of the square which holds the beads. Then the mounting cord was knotted into several overhand knots; the ends were pulled up and then threaded through the square-knot chains which were knotted to form the neck portion of the necklace. The mounting cord ends were pulled to opposite sides and included in the square-knot chains. Beads were strung onto a separate cord which was tied and looped across the mounting cord ends forming the top of the square. The portion below the four square-knot chains is simply two rows of double half hitches, a diamond with crisscrossing center cords, a fringe, and two beads added to the center cords (see detail photograph).

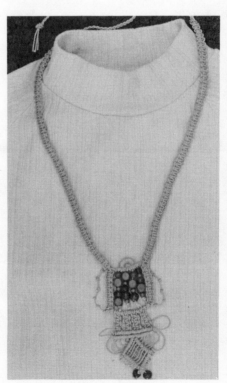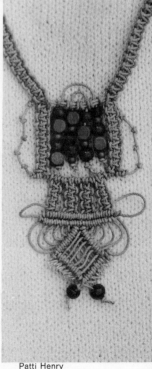

Patti Henry

COTTON TWINE with bright wooden beads makes striking necklace. (Also see inside front cover.)

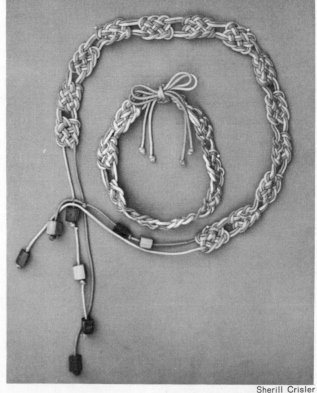

Virginia Summit

KNOTS used in these examples above are somewhat
similarly tied. At top right is Josephine knot
(page 45), at right is Oriental matting (page 47),
also see inside front cover, and above is a key
chain with a Turk's-head (page 46).
A flat variation of Turk's head is shown
at top on opposite page.

Sherill Crisler

Virginia Summit

Sally Turpie

MANY CORDS can be gathered into an attractive
plait (see purse handle above) or into simple
wrapping (see detail of necklace at right).

ADVANCED KNOTS

The variations of the two macramé knots are endless, but as your knotting capabilities and sense of design increase, you may find yourself wanting to try something different. Wrapping, advanced knots, or plaiting, used sparingly in a macramé piece can become the exclamation in a statement. But also they create a design in themselves and can easily stand alone.

Shown in this chapter are five tying methods to vary your macramé projects. The first example is wrapping, a method of finishing and concealing many cords. Most often used in jewelry and fringes, it is finding greater popularity among macramé craftsmen because it is simple and neat, yet effective. The next three—the Josephine knot, Turk's-head, and Oriental matting—are all done in somewhat the same manner. The Josephine knot and Oriental matting can add points of interest; isolated in a group of double half hitches or square knots, they introduce an element of surprise in the regularity of the macramé knots (see project, page 35). The Turk's-head can be shaped in one of three ways: flat, in a ring, or in the form of a ball. It is a good knot to use for bottle neck or drinking glass covers, for mats, or for a heavy fringe.

Plaiting, a form of braiding, is a simple and extremely attractive way of accumulating many cords into one unit.

The knot variations shown on the following pages are only a few of the numerous possibilities. A form of weaving can be created by using stationary cords (either vertical or horizontal) as the warp cords and weaving perpendicular cords through them. The central portion of the purse on the front cover illustrates this simplified form of weaving.

Another variation can be a simple braid of three cords or more which creates a flat form of plaiting. Any of the knots you have tried can be incorporated into a net-like structure by simply alternating the knots every row (the same method as alternate square-knot pattern). As an example of this knotting, next time you play tennis notice the composition of the net; or look at a hammock which is also an example of this technique. For many other advanced knot ideas, refer to the knot encyclopedias available in most libraries.

Lois Ericson

TRIM on leather vest is knotted in a freeform design with the ends gathered in wrapping.

SIMPLE WRAPPING

There are two methods of wrapping. One, which is demonstrated here, is best for small areas. The second method can be used for larger areas such as the necklace shown on page 66.

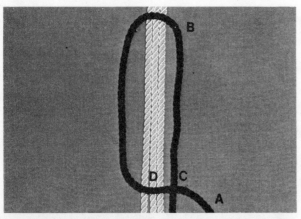

1. Cut several cords (to be wrapped) about ten inches long. Cut one cord (which will be the wrapping cord) approximately twenty inches long. Pin the ten-inch cords (D cords) to a working surface then fold the extra cord with one end slightly longer than the other end. Place this folded cord on top of the D cords. Pull end A (the long end) of the extra cord to the right side of the D cords.

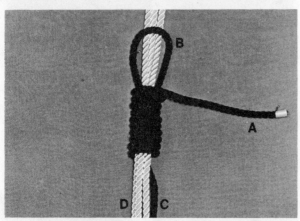

2. Begin wrapping end A around end C and all the D cords. While you are wrapping hold the cords at the point where you began wrapping. Wrap up to loop B.

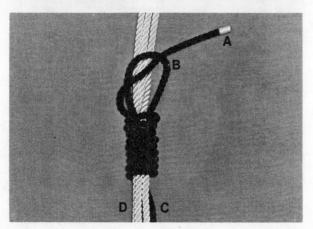

3. Thread end A through loop B. Gently pull end C until end A and loop B disappear.

The second method of wrapping is also done with a separate cord. One end of the extra cord is only folded slightly and is wrapped immediately along with all the other cords. The cord is wrapped to the very end, then the end is threaded on a large needle and sewn back into the core of the wrapping. To even wrapping, roll the piece on a hard surface.

THE JOSEPHINE KNOT

The decorative Josephine knot can be incorporated into any macramé project or can be used by itself. A belt of Josephine knots is a fast project and one which will complement any outfit.

1. Cut two cords, one gray and one white, approximately twenty inches long. Loop left cord (white) over right cord (gray). The loop will remain stationary from this point on.

2. Pull end of gray cord D over end of white cord A.

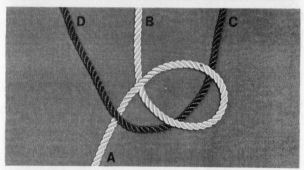

3. Pull same end of cord D under end of white cord B.

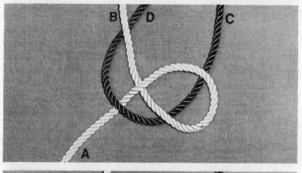

4. Bring end D down over the top side of the loop of the white cord and under cord C, where it is in the center of the loop, and then over the other side of the loop of the white cord. Leave the knot loose or pull all the ends gently to tighten the knot. Try duplicating the knot using two or more cords for each side. Keep the cords flat and parallel.

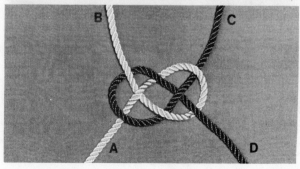

THE TURK'S-HEAD

The Turk's-head is a continuation of the Josephine knot, only it is done with just one tying cord. Once it is tied it can be a flat knot, a ring, or a tight ball. Each variation takes on a completely different appearance.

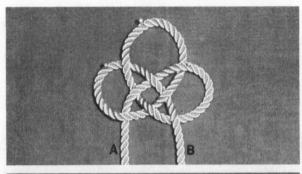

1. Cut one cord approximately thirty inches long. Fold the cord at one end leaving approximately ten inches on the right end and twenty inches on the left end. Tie the Josephine knot near the fold of the cord so the top of the fold causes a third loop.

2. Bring end A over and parallel to end B to form a fourth loop. Weave end A over, under, over, and under the loops which form the right and top side of the knot.

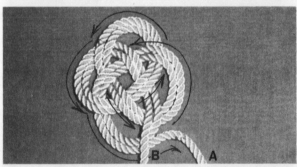

3. Continue to weave following the cord which forms the original Josephine knot until every portion of the knot has two cords. This process can be repeated many times. Just make sure that each of the interwoven loops are composed of the same number of parallel cords.

4. To form the ring, gently pull the cords out from the center. To tighten the knot into a ball, place a marble or bead in the center of the knot and gently pull all the cords until they fit snugly around the centerpiece.

ORIENTAL MATTING

Oriental matting refers to a slightly different technique of knotting in which cords are woven into a wide variety of mats, or shapes. Shown here is one simple rectangle which can be adapted to a number of uses in macramé such as coasters, placemats, jewelry, or belts.

1. Cut two cords, each thirty inches long. Fold the two cords in half, then form a loop with each by crossing over the two ends (left side cord end on top of right side cord end). Place loop C diagonally across loop F.

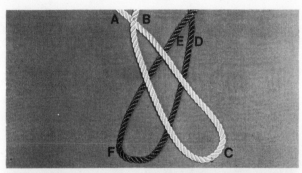

2. Pull end E of the right cord down under end D and over the two sides of loop C. Pull end E under loop F.

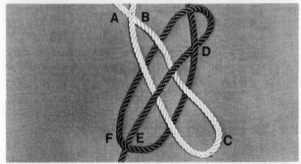

3. Bring end A down and over end B, under E, over the other end of E, under D, and over the point of loop C.

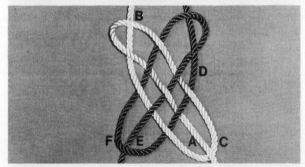

4. Gently pull the four ends one at a time until the "knot" is as tight as you would like.

To make this "knot" using just one cord, fold a cord in half, then make two loops near the center with the two loose ends. Ignore the top loop and proceed using the same steps as for two cords.

FOUR CORD
ROUND PLAITING

There are many forms of plaiting and although they look complicated, they are merely a form of braiding. Plaiting is useful in any portion of a piece where you might like to gather all the cords into one attractive unit. Plaiting is a good way of making a simple belt or a sturdy handle for a purse.

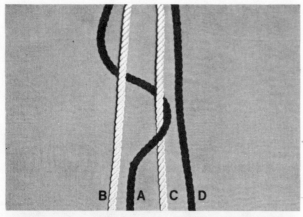

1. Start with four cords (two black and two white). Put one black cord on either side of the two white cords. Pull the left outside cord A under both B and C. Then pull it over C, letting it hang vertically in the space between the two cords B and C.

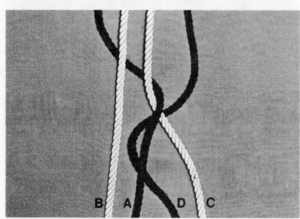

2. Take the right outside cord D and repeat the same process by pulling D under A and C. Then pull D over A, letting D hang vertically in the space between A and C.

3. Take cord B and pull it under A and D, then over D, letting it hang vertically in the space between A and D.

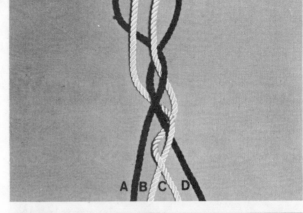

4. Take cord C, put it under B and D, then over B, letting it hang vertically between B and D. Notice that only three cords are used in any one step.

5. Continue in this pattern always alternating between the left outside cord and the right outside cord until the desired length has been reached.

6. To achieve a completely different appearance, switch the positions of the colors, pinning two white cords on the left and two black cords on the right.

7. Repeat the above instructions making sure you always alternate between the left outside cord and right outside cord while you braid. Then compare this plait to the first.

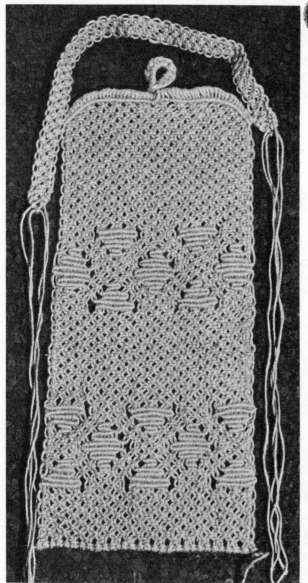

Gerta Wingerd

HANDBAG can be knotted in one piece, then handle can be attached along sides (see unfinished bag at left and purse above). A belt can be started from center, worked to ends (see example below).

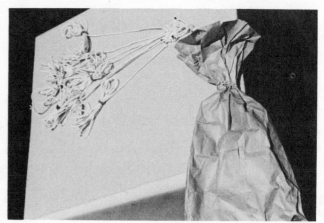

Mary E. Anderson

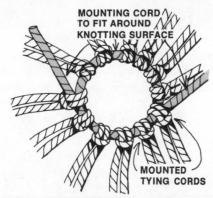

MOUNTING CORD TO FIT AROUND KNOTTING SURFACE

MOUNTED TYING CORDS

MOUNTING CORDS on strand held in a circle is simple way to adjust cords around knotting surface. The two mounting cord ends can be pulled tightly.

Virginia Summit

GENERAL TECHNIQUES

FRINGE is held by Turk's head.

As you develop your macramé skills, you will discover techniques that work well for you. You will become adept at picking the appropriate working surface, at selecting beginnings and endings that complement your macramé piece, and at choosing proper fastenings for the project. You will become proficient at adding on to short cords and at adding cords to introduce color or to increase the size of a piece. As you become more confident of your knotting ability and your working techniques, you may want to attempt three-dimensional pieces. On the following pages, three kinds of projects—belts, handbags, and jewelry—are used to illustrate different techniques which can make your knotting easier and more enjoyable.

• **PREPARING A WORKING SURFACE.** There are many working surfaces and types of mountings to consider when designing a belt, a bag, or jewelry. The suggestions which follow can be adapted to nearly every macramé project you attempt.

A belt can be worked on almost any surface (see page 7) or can even be knotted without being secured to a board. If the cord ends are held in a vice attached to a stable surface or closed securely into a drawer, the cords will be taut enough for knotting.

Handbags need to be pinned securely to a working surface. The kind of working surface depends on the shape of the bag. There are basically four different ways of shaping a bag: knotting continuously around with no side seams, knotting two separate pieces to be seamed on three sides, knotting one long piece which is folded and then seamed on the sides, and securing one or two pieces with a handle attached to the sides (see unfinished bag at left). If you are working a continuous knotted pattern, slip your circular mounted cords over an oatmeal box (see example at bottom left) or around a piece of plywood cut to the width of the bag. Once the pattern has been knotted to the correct length, slip the bag off the box or board and flatten it with an iron. The other three shapes can be worked on a regular flat surface.

Jewelry requires relatively little cord and little knotting space. The best surface to use is a small piece of ceiling tile or foam rubber which will accommodate many pins. In general, jewelry is best worked flat to a board; however it is better to work necklaces around a wig stand, or even on a dress form.

• **BEGINNINGS AND ENDINGS.** Belts can have a variety of beginnings and endings. They can be worked from the center or from end to end; they can be mounted or unmounted. To begin a belt from the center, place half the cord ends in a bag. Pin the second half to a working surface and begin knotting at the center point (see photograph at far left). When one side is knotted, remove the cord ends from the bag and, beginning at the center, repeat the knotting process. Some of the projects on pages 32 and 34 were worked in this manner.

Fringe is the natural result of leaving your knotted piece unfinished at the ends. To prevent unraveling and to add a decorative touch to the fringe, tie an overhand knot or Turk's-head ring as shown above (see page 46), or knot a restraining bar of double half hitches.

A pointed end can be created from mounted or

unmounted cords. The first group of illustrations (below) shows the unmounted method—first tie a square knot using two cords looped and pinned at the center. Then pin two more cords slightly below and to either side of the square knot and tie two more square knots using the cords of the first knot as well. The second method is shown in the photograph and the illustrations below. Tie several cords in double half hitches to a horizontal cord. Then tie a square knot with the four center cords and pull the two sides down into diagonals to form the point. To secure this position, tie two more square knots below and to either side of the center square knot. The ends with which you finish your knotting can be sewn, glued, or tied onto a buckle, ring, or support of some kind.

Handbags lend themselves well to a number of beginnings and endings. Like the belt, a handbag can have a pointed end which serves as the flap of the purse (see photograph at right).

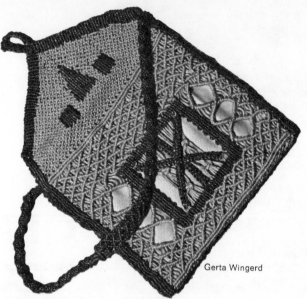

PURSES can have pointed flap which would be started in the same manner as the belts, with mounted or unmounted cords.

Gerta Wingerd

FORMING POINTED END, METHOD I

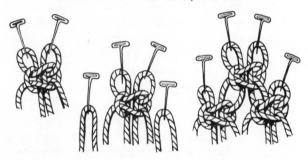

TIE one square knot, then tie two square knots below and to either side to create point.

For a decorative heading on a bag which begins on a mounting cord, an example is shown below. To form the scallops, mount a cord and pull it up above the mounting cord. Using one cord end as a holding cord and the other cord end as a tying cord, knot several half hitches. Then curve the knotted section into a scallop above the mounting cord (see illustration). Bring the two ends under the mounting cord and tie double half hitches with each end onto the mounting cord. Mount additional cords in the center of the scallop and to the sides to fill the space of the top row on the bag.

FORMING POINTED END, METHOD II

Virginia Summit

MOUNTED CORDS pulled into diagonals form a point which can be secured by knotting directly below the mounting cord.

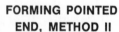

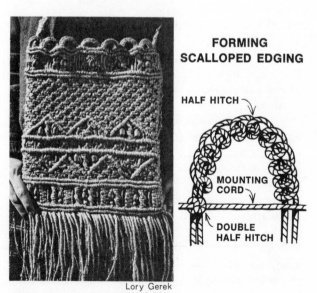

Lory Gerek

PICOTS are the small scallops which decorate the mounting bar on this purse.

FORMING SCALLOPED EDGING

HALF HITCH

MOUNTING CORD

DOUBLE HALF HITCH

The heading of a bag does not have to be ornate. The loose mounting of the cords shown on the purse below blends well with the overall casualness of the pattern on the bag.

As in the two bags pictured below, the endings can be simply a heavy fringe hanging from the seamed bottom. For a flat bottom (see purse shown at right), knot a continuous pattern around a board. Shape the bottom into four points as illustrated (alternate square-knot pattern, page 27, is a good way to create the points). When you take the bag from the working surface, slip a piece of cardboard or wood cut to the size of the bottom of the purse (see illustration) into place just above the points as a permanent bottom. Or you can cut the bottom off of a large plastic bleach bottle and use it as a permanent reinforcement for the purse bottom. Sew or knot all four points together, then weave the ends into the inside of the bag.

Jewelry can be started at any point and can therefore have a variety of beginnings and endings. Necklaces can be started from the neck and knotted down to the main portion or vice versa. They can also be started from both ends at once and worked to a central portion, from a central point, or from a found object. Necklaces and neckpieces are good projects on which to practice adding on cords (see instructions, page 56). A pendant necklace can have the neckpiece formed by a length of wrapping (see page 66) which is pulled into a circle. The pendant can then be started from cords mounted onto the wrapped neckpiece.

Headings and fringes on jewelry can be enhanced by the addition of beads or knots. Fringes with the

SHAPING FOR FLAT BOTTOMED PURSE

PERMANENT BOTTOM

POINTED END

Lester H. Henley

ENDS are knotted to form four points and are then sewn together to form flat bottom of purse

ends tied in overhand knots (try variation shown on page 12) or knotted in delicate half-knot chains gives a finished touch to the piece.

Chokers can be knotted in the same manner as a belt, from one end to the other or from the center out. The fringed ends can be decreased into chains or can be clipped off and tacked under.

• FASTENINGS. Fastenings for belts and jewelry are particularly challenging. Plan how you want the belt or jewelry to fasten before you begin the project.

An easy fastening for a belt is two rings held together by the mounted cords. The end of the belt can be pulled through the rings as shown in the photograph below.

Christie Gibson

FREEFORM DESIGN of this handbag complements the loose mounting and heavy fringe.

Linda Weingarten

TWO HEAVY RINGS, on which cords were mounted, secure the end of belt.

A MACRAME BELT can be started from a point, then the buckle can be attached on the opposite end. For a secure fastening use any knot pattern which will yield regular holes for prong of buckle.

If the cords are mounted on a buckle, a tightly knotted alternate square-knot pattern or spaced rows of double half hitches yield regular holes just right for the prong of a buckle (see photograph above). For a fastening without the buckle, knot one end of a belt in alternate square-knot chains then tie bobbles on the opposite end at intervals corresponding to the spaces between the chains. Then button the bobbles through the holes (see photograph below).

A third example of a belt fastening is pictured at right. Begin knotting on a drapery ring and tie the cords loosely into an "X" pattern of double half hitches. To fasten the belt, pull the end through and back over the edge of the ring (see illustration). Then bring it back to a point on the belt where a large oblong button is sewn in place. Pull the button through the gap between the two "X's" to secure the belt. ‹

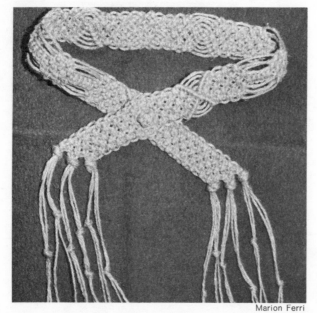

FASTENING FOR A BELT

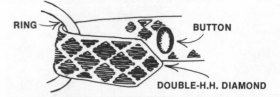

RING — BUTTON

DOUBLE-H.H. DIAMOND

DIAMOND PATTERN on belt above leaves spaces where large button can be pulled through. Belt at left, done with alternate square knots and chains, allows opening large enough for square-knot bobble.

Fastenings for a macramé purse are not necessary but if you want to add one, there are several ways to do it. The cords can be mounted on a handle purchased in a weaving or crafts store; these handles normally come with a lock as shown in the photograph at right. Or a small chain of knots can be attached to one edge of the purse, then buttoned to the other edge (see example below). A bag can be drawn up at the edge by attaching rings along the top of the knotting. The handle can then be made of round plaiting or of some macramé chain and threaded through the rings (see example of plaited handle on bag, page 42). A flap with a loop at the point is another form of fastening (see purse, page 52).

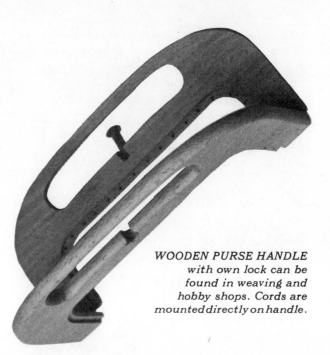

WOODEN PURSE HANDLE
*with own lock can be
found in weaving and
hobby shops. Cords are
mounted directly on handle.*

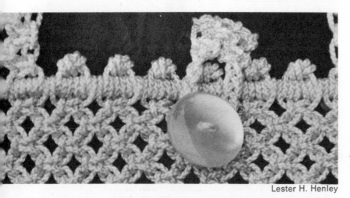

Lester H. Henley

*CORDS FOLDED AND BRAIDED at center can form
loop for a button. Then two braids can be knotted
together into square-knot chain.*

Macramé necklaces can be made large enough to be pulled over your head without any fastenings, can be started on a metal ring which hooks in the back, or can be finished with a loop and bead which fastens the two ends (see photograph at right). The holding cords for this necklace were pulled through the hole of the bead. A separate (different colored) cord was knotted over all these holding cords in a square-knot chain. The loop side of the neckpiece was formed by first folding two cords in half. At the central point, one of the cords was used as a tying cord, the other as a holding cord—several half hitches were tied to form the loop. The ends (two cords on each end) were then knotted in a square-knot chain over several center cords. The two sides of the neckpiece were knotted to the point where the main portion of the necklace began. All the holding cords and tying cords from each side were knotted into this main portion.

Fastenings for choker necklaces and bracelets can be done in the same manner as the watch band shown on page 33. A choker started and finished on two small rings can be attached by threading a ribbon through the rings and tying the choker onto your neck. You can glue under or weave back the ends of a choker and then sew snaps or hooks and eyes to the wrong side of the choker at the ends.

Joyce Barnes

*LOOP, formed in the same way as picots, can be
adjusted to fit any bead for a fastening.*

● ADDING ON CORDS. If you should run out of cord at a vital point in your project, there are several ways to solve the problem. Shown in the illustrations below are methods of adding to a short tying or holding cord in the double half hitch and the square knot.

A new color or cord can be easily added into a project. The vertical double half hitch is an excellent knot to use when spots of color are needed. Using a tying cord of a different color from the holding cords allows you to introduce the color and then hide it at any point by tying some regular double half hitches. When you do not want to vary the knots or would like to add onto square knots as well, the best methods of adding color or enlarging a piece are those shown below.

ADDING TO SHORT CORD

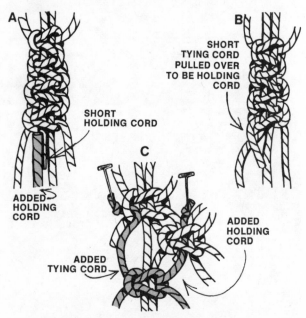

TO ADD onto short holding cord, pin new cord alongside short holding cord; knot over both.
To replace short tying cord, add second holding cord which drops to become tying cord.

IN SQUARE KNOT, (A) added holding cord is knotted in; (B) one of the holding cords becomes tying cord while short tying cord becomes holding cord; (C) new cords can be added directly where needed.

INCREASING SIZE AND ADDING COLOR

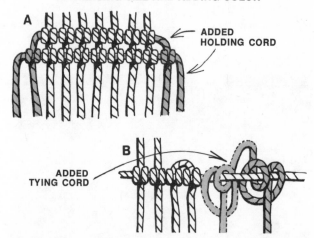

ADD HOLDING CORD in each row, always knotting ends into next row, see A. Put folded tying cord under holding cord; tie each end in double half hitch, see B.

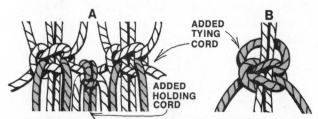

WEAVE new cords into square knot; pull two tying cords to center, secure with new cord mounted on them, see A. Square knot cord onto any cords, see B.

● WORKING IN THREE DIMENSIONS. Working macramé into three dimensions or onto a three-dimensional surface requires some preliminary planning and basic understanding of design. A three-dimensional piece can be viewed from several angles and must be satisfying from each view.

Shown in some of the following photographs are just a few of the items you can use to mount cords to create a three-dimensional piece. Embroidery rings are excellent forms on which to start a piece, but other possible articles could be a bamboo trivet or candle holders. Remember that unless you add on cords, the size of your macramé will correspond to the size of the mounting piece. The three-dimensional piece shown at right was started on a small hoop. As additional cords were needed, a larger hoop was tied in with double half hitches using the existing cord ends as well as added cords.

Covering an existing three-dimensional piece is often easier than creating a three-dimensional shape yourself. Lamp shades, flower pots, and bottles are just a few possible surfaces. Bottles are popular items to decorate. The knotting on a bottle can be started from a circular mounting cord (see illustration, page 50) which is pulled around the neck of the bottle. The knots must be consistent, and eventually cords must be added to increase the number of cord ends. Two examples of bottle covers are shown below. The necks were knotted with the alternate square-knot pattern. Once the bottom of the bottle was reached, a spiral of double half hitches coming into the center was tied. The cords were clipped as the spiral got smaller and smaller, and the loose ends were tucked into the inside of the knotting between the bottle and the macramé. Remember to keep your knots evenly spaced and tight. Add on cords when your pattern begins to stretch out of shape. When determining the length of cords, remember that the curve of the bottle requires longer cords than are necessary for a straight-sided piece.

Jacee Johnson

MACRAMÉ TIERS grow bigger with addition of larger rings. Cords must be added each time.

CANDLEHOLDERS

BAMBOO TRIVET

HOUSEHOLD ITEMS are good three-dimensional supports for projects.

Alison Jones

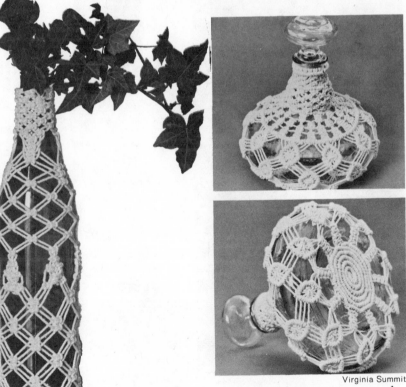

Virginia Summit

OLD BOTTLES become new decanters with macramé covering. Begin knotting at the neck.

BARK ON AGED PALM TREE casts shadows and has ridges which suggest the tight knotting of sculptural hanging shown at right. (Also see inside back cover.)

Sachi Honmyo

Marion Ferri

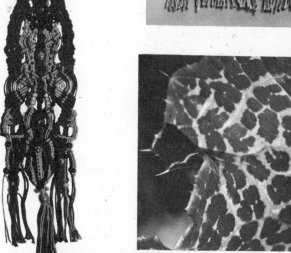

USE OF COLOR in this delicate hanging resembles the variegated leaf shown above. See page 61 for transferring of color.

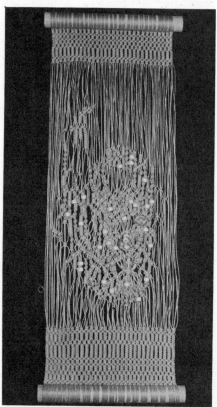

Marion Ferri

UNKNOTTED CORDS give appearance of falling water.

Mary E. Anderson

DESIGN AND COLOR IDEAS

SHAPE of temple can be inspiration for macramé hanging.

After you have decided to try a macramé project of your own design, there are several criteria to consider before beginning a piece. This chapter covers project planning, some elementary instruction in design, and the use of color in your macramé projects.

• PLANNING THE PROJECT. A few questions logically precede the actual process of beginning a project. What shall I make? What size should it be? What color or colors would be best to use? What materials would be most suitable? Keep the size and complexity of the project in line with your capabilities and the amount of time you want to spend on it. Use colors that complement your macramé piece as well as the items seen with or next to it.

Your decisions on project, size, and colors will help you to determine which materials to use. If you decide, for example, to make a macramé drapery for a window, consider those materials that are thick enough so the knotting process will not take months for you to complete the piece. The materials should also be colorfast to prevent fading in the sunlight. Reds and blues have a greater tendency to fade than some of the more neutral colors. The planning can seem less important to you than the knotting process; however, many mistakes can be prevented if the project is well-thought-out.

• DESIGNING A MACRAMÉ PROJECT. Design is just as important to your macramé project as the knots themselves. A well-planned macramé piece combines all the elements of design into a harmonious whole which would be incomplete if anything were added or taken away. Design can be broken down into basic elements of line, shape, and space. These three elements are found in nature as well as in things which often go unnoticed around us. Find

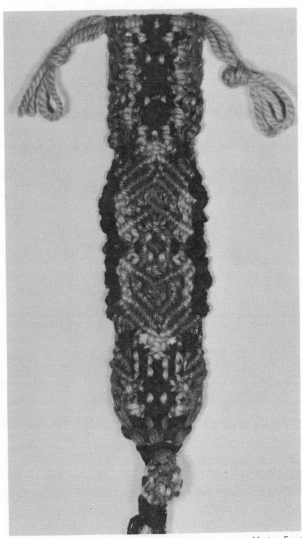

Marion Ferri

BELL PULL shows how to move and redistribute color in macramé. (Also see back cover.)

line in the cascading water of a fall, shape in the elaborate configurations of a temple, and space in the delicate web of a spider. These three elements are defined further by repetition, texture, and contrast. Repetition in your macramé can bring interest through the repeated use of one element. Texture comes from the knots as well as the material you chose, and contrast is a comparison of two radically different elements. When you feel you understand these design elements, try applying them in your macramé in a way that creates simplicity and continuity in the piece. A good exercise is to find something in nature, then try to duplicate it exactly with the macramé knots you have learned. By concentrating on the minute details of an object of nature, your eye will be trained to see all the elements which make up the object you chose.

• WORKING COLOR INTO YOUR MACRAMÉ.

Color is a very personal aspect of overall design. Often people have a natural sense of color without knowing any of the color rules. It is not necessary to memorize rules, but it is important to have a basic knowledge of what color is, what it can be, and how you can apply it to macramé. Understanding the composition of colors gives you confidence and control of your medium and allows you to employ colors so that they work well in your macramé projects.

COLOR WHEEL

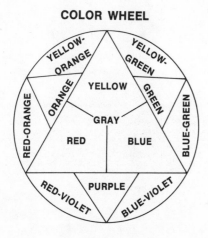

Color is best understood in terms of a color wheel (pictured above). The wheel positions colors in an order which shows how each color is produced and how each color relates to one another. The three primary colors are yellow, red, and blue. When two primary colors are combined, a secondary color is produced. Yellow with red creates orange; red with blue creates purple; blue with yellow creates green. As one example of how this principle works in macramé, experiment by twisting several yarns of

red and yellow together. You will find that the resulting piece appears to be orange. A third group of colors (tertiary) on the wheel is created by mixing the adjacent primary and secondary colors.

The color wheel has what is termed a warm and cool side. Oranges and reds are considered warm colors, blues and greens cool colors. Try combining cords of different colors to create a mood, temperature, or movement.

The actual mechanics of including color in your work can be accomplished by three methods: adding (tying in color at any point in your macramé as illustrated on page 56), moving, and redistributing color. The last two are achieved by working with cords and colors you started with. A small sampler, which can be made into a decorative bell pull, is explained here to demonstrate techniques of moving color in macramé projects (also see back cover).

• USING COLOR IN A BELL PULL.

The following project is presented to encourage the use of color, to help you understand how color can be manipulated, and to assist you in achieving different effects in your macramé projects. The colors used in the following example are mounted in a particular order, and after relatively few knots, the color positions are completely reversed. Eventually they return to their original order. These changes occur by making a 1½ square knot (which changes positions of the cords from one side to the other) and by knotting rows of different lengths of diagonal double half hitches. The bell pull is divided into three portions; each section accentuates certain colors by the way the square knots are tied, by the overhand knots, and by the use of bobbles. Some colors are hidden by using the cords as holding cords in both the square knots and double half hitches.

To begin, cut a piece of heavy cord for a mounting cord and tie overhand knots at each end; pin the cord to your working surface. Cut eight cords (two each of four different colors) approximately 4½ yards long. The colors used in the bell pull are orange, gold, yellow, and yellow-green. You can use the same colors or four other colors of your choice. The cords will be referred to on the chart by numbers: 1 for orange, 2 for gold, 3 for yellow, and 4 for yellow-green.

Fold each cord in half and mount them on the mounting cord in this order: 1,2,3,4,4,3,2,1. It might help to pin the assigned number above each cord on the mounting cord.

You will notice on the chart that there are numbers above as well as directly below the symbol for the knot. The numbers above denote the order of the cords used in the knots. The numbers below denote the order of the cords as they emerge from the knot. In order to make your bell pull exactly as the one shown here, be sure to tie your square knots in the same direction as shown (see legend for definition of symbols).

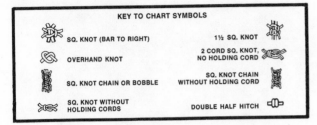

SECTION I

First, knot three rows of alternate square knots using two tying cords and two holding cords for each knot. Row one is four knots of the combination 1,1,2,2; 3,3,4,4; 4,4,3,3; 2,2,1,1. Row two is three knots of the combination 2,2,3,3; 4,4,4,4; 3,3,2,2. Row three is a repeat of row one (notice that the two center square knots are tied differently). At this point the order of the cords has not changed from their original position. In the fourth row, knot three groups of 1½ square knots (one square knot with one half knot) with cords 2,2,3,3; 4,4,4,4; 3,3,2,2 which will then position the cords into 3,2,3,2; 4,4,4,4; 2,3,2,3. In row five, knot 1½ square knots with the four outside cords on either side 1,1,3,2 and 2,3,1,1 which positions these cords into 2,1,3,1 and 1,3,1,2. Skip the two cords 3,3 on either side and tie three square knots without holding cords using 2,4; 4,4; 4,2. Directly below these three square knots, tie a row of four square knots without holding cords using 3,2; 4,4; 4,4; 2,3. Row six is a series of square knots using all the cords. On both sides, knot two square knots without holding cords with cords 2,1; 3,1; and 1,3; 1,2. Tie the middle two square knots with four cords in each knot (3,2,4,4—left, and 4,4,2,3—right). The seventh row has the bobble in it. First tie a square knot without holding cords with cords 2,1 on the left and 1,2 on the right. Next to these knots, tie 1½ square knots with cords 3,1,3,2 and 2,3,1,3 which positions these cords into 2,1,3,3 and 3,3,1,2. To tie the bobble, knot four square knots using the middle four cords 4,4,4,4. Pull the holding cords over the top of the four square knots and take them through the space between the holding cords. Pull ends down firmly and secure the bobble with a final square knot. With the second and third cords on both sides (2,1 and 1,2), tie a double half hitch using cord 1 as a diagonal holding cord and 2 as the tying cord. Skip the cords 1,1 and 1,1 on each side. Knot 1½ square knots beneath the bobble using cords 3,3,4,4

for the left knot and cords 4,4,3,3 for the right knot which positions these cords into 4,3,4,3 and 3,4,3,4. Tie an overhand knot with two outside cords 2,2 on each side. Then tie a double half hitch using 3 as a holding cord and 4 as a tying cord. This is the completion of the first section. The cord positions are now: 2,2,1,1,4,4,3,3,3,3,4,4,1,1,2,2. Notice how the alternate square-knot pattern gives an overall peppering effect of color and how the bobble concentrates one color into a small area.

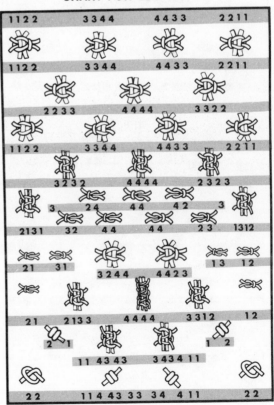

Marion Ferri

DETAIL OF BELL PULL shows first section from the mounting bar to row nine.

CHART FOR SECTION I

SECTION II

The second section shows how to redistribute and accentuate certain colors. Begin this section by tying three 1½ square knots with cords 2,2,1,1,4,4 on the left; 3,3,3,3 in the center; and 4,4,1,1,2,2 on the right. The new position of the cords is 4,2,1,1, 4,2,3,3,3,3,2,4,1,1,2,4. Below this row, pull cords 4,4 (the ones nearest the center) across cords 1,1,2,4 on the left and across 1,1,2,4 on the right toward the edges. Knot a diagonal bar of double half hitches on cord 4. Pull the two center cords 3,3 into a diagonal next to the first row of double half hitches and knot a second bar using 3 as holding cord and 3,2,1,1,2 as tying cords. Knot a third diagonal row of double half hitches using the next center cords 3,3 as holding cords and 2,1,1,2,3 as tying cords. Tie the final diagonal row, crossing over the cords 2 and 2 and using them as holding cords with 1,1,2 as tying cords. With the loose ends of 4,4 on each side, tie four overhand knots. With the two ends of 3,3 on

Marion Ferri

SECOND SECTION shows colors completely reversed from their order in row one.

each side, knot two square knots without holding cords. Knot one square knot without a holding cord on each side with cords 2,2 and 2,2. Knot the center cords 1,1,1,1 into two square knots tied without a holding cord. Notice how at this point the order of the cords is completely reversed from the order at the beginning of section I of the sampler.

Next a diamond will be formed by first pulling the two center cords 1,1 to a diagonal and tying double half hitches on them with cords 1,2,2,3,3,4,4 on each side. To accentuate the point on either side of the diamond, tie an overhand knot with cord 1 at the end of the row of double half hitches. Fill in the center of the diamond by first tying a square knot with the four middle cords 2,1,1,2. Then tie one square knot below and on either side using 3,2,2,1 on the left and 1,2,2,3 on the right. Tie the third row of square knots with 4,3,3,2 and 2,3,3,4. To form the center of the diamond, tie three square knots with 1,1 without holding cords. Knot one square knot below and to either side of the center knot with cords 3,2,2,1 on the left and 1,2,2,3 on the right. Tie a final square knot for the center portion of the diamond with the center four cords 2,1,1,2. To form the bottom half of the diamond, pull both cords 1 back to the center and knot double half hitches with 4,4,3,3,2,2,1 and 1. Repeat the entire pattern above the diamond, working backwards to the beginning of section two, but remember to slant all the diagonal double half hitches downward and toward the center.

CHART FOR SECTION II

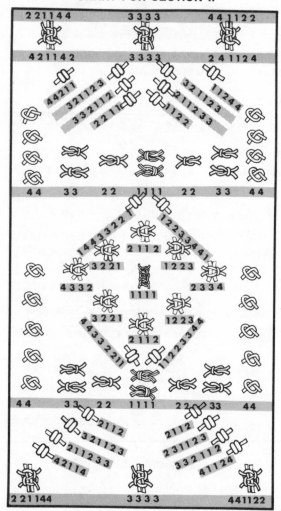

This section is completed in the same way as it was started, with three square knots. Notice at this point how color can be moved from one side to the other by the use of diagonal double half hitches.

SECTION III

The third and final section of the bell pull shows another peppering of color as well as areas of one concentrated color. A large bobble predominates the bottom section with all the warm colors held into a tight group by the green cords.

Starting below the row of square knots (section II), pull the two outside cords 2,2 diagonally into the center. Knot double half hitches on it with cords 2,1,1. Pull the next outside cord 2 below the first diagonal bar and knot a second row of double half hitches with 1,1,2. Near the center, knot 1½ square knots with cords 4,4,3,3 and 3,3,4,4. Tie one square knot with the two central cords 4,4 and then knot a square knot on each side with 3,4,3,4 and 4,3,4,3. At this point, the order of the central cords changes by crossing 4,3 on the left and 3,4 on the right. The position of the cords becomes 3,3,4,4 and 4,4,3,3. Knot another single square knot with cords 4,4,4,4 below the two square knot chains. Tie a square knot on either side of this center knot using cords 2,2,3,3 for the left and 3,3,2,2 for the right. With outside cords 1,1 and 1,1, knot 1½ square knots without holding cords. Below this row, knot a row of four square knots using 1,1,2,2; 3,3,4,4; 4,4,3,3; 2,2,1,1. Beneath this row tie three square

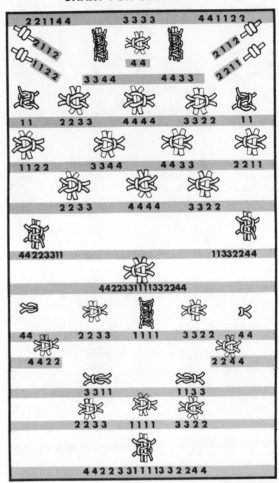

CHART FOR SECTION III

knots using 2,2,3,3; 4,4,4,4; 3,3,2,2; skip the outside cords 1. Coming into the final section of the sampler, tie two groups of 1½ square knots using 1,1 and 4,4 as tying cords and all the other cords as holding cords. Next tie a square knot using 4,4,4,4 as tying cords and all the other cords as holding cords—pull the knot tightly. Tie four square knots without a holding cord using cords 1,1,1,1. On both sides of this chain, knot a square knot using cords 2,2,3,3 and 3,3,2,2. Turn the entire project over and knot one square knot with cords 4,4,4,4. Turn the project back over and knot a square knot on the left with 4,4,2,2 and one on the right with 2,2,4,4. With cords 3,3,1,1 on the left and 1,1,3,3 on the right, tie two square knots without a holding cord. Below these two knots, tie three square knots with cords 2,2,3,3; 1,1,1,1; 3,3,2,2. Finish this section by knotting one square knot with 4,4,4,4 as tying cords and the remaining cords as holding cords. Pull the knot tightly. Examine your completed project and analyze which effects you like. Incorporate your favorite ways of using color into your project designs.

Marion Ferri

FINAL SECTION is made of many small square knots. Bell can be tied under prominent bobble.

DESIGN AND COLOR **63**

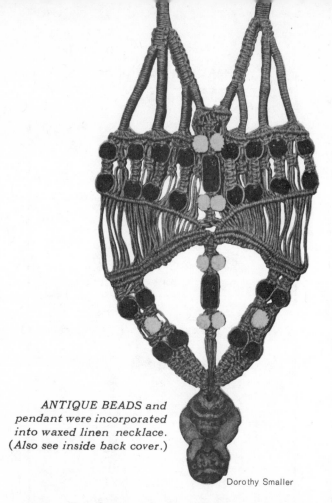

ANTIQUE BEADS and
pendant were incorporated
into waxed linen necklace.
(Also see inside back cover.)

Dorothy Smaller

Lois Ericson

LEATHER CAPE is adorned with macramé fringe.
Cords are mounted in holes punched in leather.

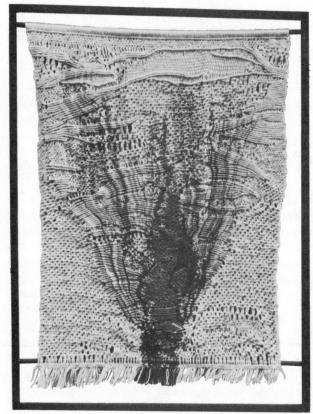

Marion Ferri

Kathleen M. Ratigan

WALL HANGING shows effect of added color. Purse
contrasts tight patterns with carefree fringe.

Marion Ferri

ALLACIARE (HANGING) has movement of color, interlacing of cords. (Also see inside back cover.)

Susan Lehman

INDIAN-LIKE hanging was started from ring then tied in circular rows of double half hitches.

INGENUITY IN MACRAMÉ

The pace of twentieth-century progress has forced most of us to accept the necessity of mass production. Since the majority of products we purchase today are machine made in large quantities, it is understandable in the new emerging awareness of human needs that the work of the craftsman is acclaimed and idolized. Today only the craftsman working with his hands has the satisfaction of producing a one-of-a-kind, loved, and labored-over creation.

Macramé is dependent upon the willingness and patience of the craftsman's hands. It requires no tools to carry the threads and therefore truly becomes a personal work of the artist. Macramé can be worked into free-flowing, uninhibited forms or into tight, exacting patterns. Yet, no matter how precise a piece, it still has the unique inconsistencies characteristic of anything made by hand.

The variety of modern materials, ever changing modes of design, and unlimited knot combinations make macramé a versatile art medium which encourages experimentation and imagination from amateur and professional craftsmen alike. With its growing popularity, macramé has evolved from tassels and small adornments into massive as well as minute individual works of art.

This chapter is for the macramé enthusiast who feels, after completing a few projects, that he is ready to design and create some original pieces. The ideas here are presented as inspiration rather than as structured goals. When developing your design, decide on a theme or direction and carry it throughout your piece. (For some design suggestions refer to the chapter on page 59.) With self-confidence and control of the medium, you can transform your thoughts and motivations into admirable macramé compositions.

Dorothy Smaller

NECKPIECE of necklace is simple wrapping. (Also see inside back cover).

Sally Turpie

WHITE FEATHERS *contrast with deep purple necklace done in alternate square-knot pattern (see detail of necklace at left).*

Lois Ericson

Rosa Leeson

CHILD'S SWEATER *(above) was knotted not knitted. (Also see inside back cover.) Tied with bright colored yarn, a necklace can be as simple as six rows of double half hitches and a long fringe (left).*

Joyce Barnes

Joyce Barnes

NECKLACES are so natural they give impression of having grown rather than having been constructed.

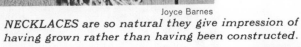

Gerta Wingerd

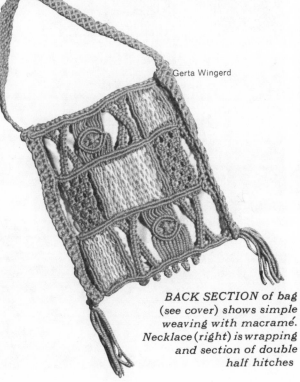

Sally Turpie

BACK SECTION of bag (see cover) shows simple weaving with macramé. Necklace (right) is wrapping and section of double half hitches

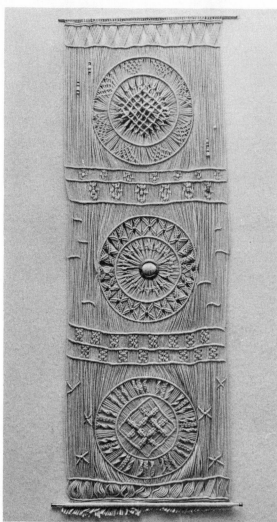

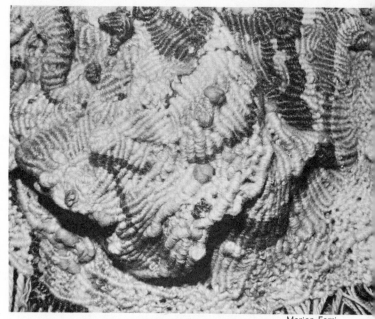

Marion Ferri

DRAPERY FOR DOORWAY (left) presents complex
problem of working the cords into center of each
circle then out again. Detail of unfinished
hanging, Meteora, (above) shows sculptural
quality created by "over-knotting" a given area.
(Also see inside back cover.)

Virginia Summit

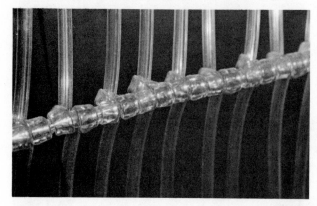

*PLASTIC TUBING makes a sturdy room divider.
With just the use of double half-hitch bars and
no other knotting, simplicity is quite elegant.
Photograph above shows detail of knotting.
Tubing can be purchased from medical suppliers.*

Hella Berg

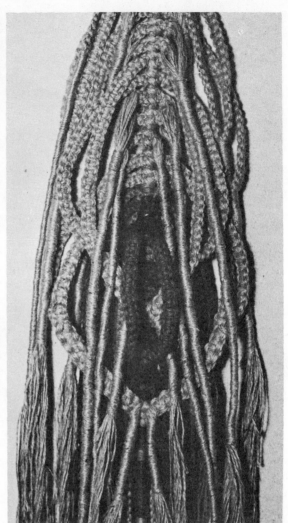

ROOM DIVIDER (above) is almost 10 ft. x 15 ft. For
color view of hanging (right) see inside back cover.

Joyce Newcomb

Donna Armstrong

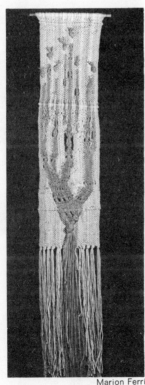

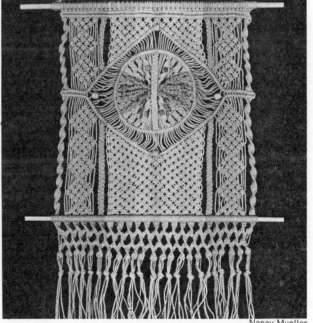

Marion Ferri

Nancy Mueller

MENORAH SHAPE is formed by added color.
Hanging (right) has alternate half-knot chain fringe.

INGENUITY IN MACRAMÉ **69**

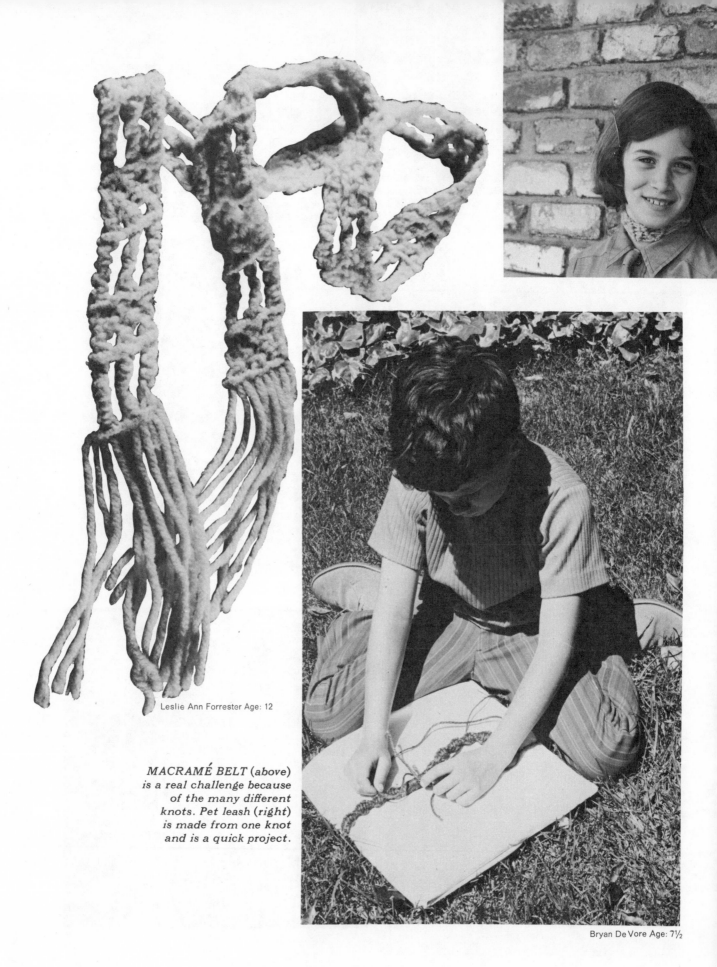

Leslie Ann Forrester Age: 12

*MACRAMÉ BELT (above)
is a real challenge because
of the many different
knots. Pet leash (right)
is made from one knot
and is a quick project.*

Bryan De Vore Age: 7½

Claire Frawley Age: 8
Crystal Kooyers Age: 8

A HEADBAND or choker, page 60.

MACRAMÉ FOR CHILDREN

The macramé projects in this chapter are especially geared for children seven to twelve years old. Each piece has simple instructions and an illustration for each step. Most of the knotting can be done by children themselves but some help may be needed from an adult. Only a few pieces of equipment and a few materials are necessary: a hard throw pillow or a piece of ceiling tile, five to six T-pins, scissors, tape measure, cotton rug yarn, jute, or cotton seine twine, and some extras such as beads, drapery rings, and ribbon. (See illustrations at right.)

• **TO THE CHILDREN:** There are a few things to remember while you are practicing knots or working on a project. Always pin or hold securely the cords which will not be moved during the knotting. When you tie a knot, pull it tight but not so tight you can barely see the shape of the knot. Follow the instructions and illustrations carefully. If you do not understand how to do one of the knots, practice it with some extra cord or get an adult to help you. After you have tried some of the projects, think how you might knot a bookmarker for your father or a potholder for your mother using the knots you have learned.

If you would like to learn more about macramé, turn to page 12 and begin practicing the knots shown there.

• **TO THE PARENTS:** After the children have tried some of the projects in this section, possibly they could learn the basic macramé knots described on pages 12 through 27. Children can often learn the two basic macramé knots (half hitch and square knot), then go on to create amazing and complex designs. Let the children attempt to do things by themselves so they can discover the style and methods of knotting which appeal to them alone.

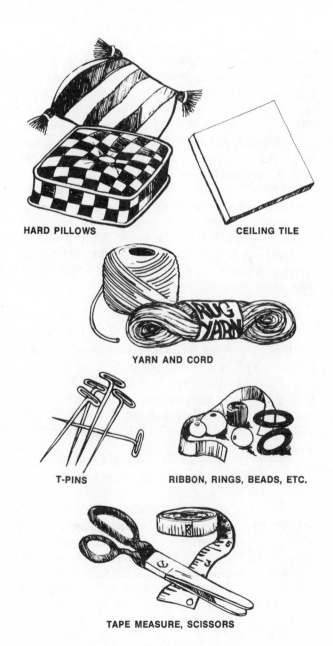

HARD PILLOWS

CEILING TILE

YARN AND CORD

T-PINS

RIBBON, RINGS, BEADS, ETC.

TAPE MEASURE, SCISSORS

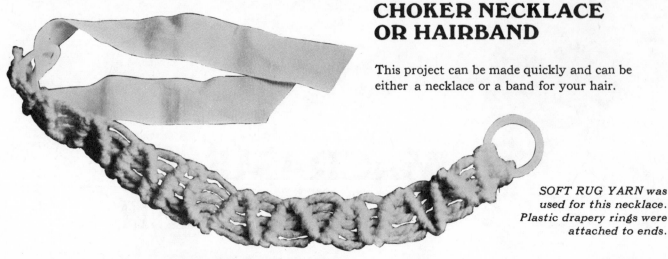

CHOKER NECKLACE OR HAIRBAND

This project can be made quickly and can be either a necklace or a band for your hair.

SOFT RUG YARN was used for this necklace. Plastic drapery rings were attached to ends.

1. To start, pin a small plastic drapery ring to your working surface. Choose a soft yarn, then cut four cords each eight times longer than the measurement around your neck or head. Fold each piece of yarn in half and put the folded piece of yarn with loop A in the middle of the ring as shown at right.

2. Pull the loop A over the ring and down next to the two ends of yarn B and C. Then pull the ends B and C up through loop A. Pull the ends until the knot is tight around the ring.

3. Do this same knot with the three cords you have left (see illustration at right).

4. Take cord B and pull it across the other cords C,D,E,F,G,H,I. Pin cord B below the ring and to the right side of cord I as shown at right. (Instead of pinning B to the right side you could hold it with your right hand while you tie the loops with your left hand.)

5. Take cord C and bring it up over B, then back down behind B. Do the same thing with C again, bringing it up over B, back around, then through the loop. This is knot number one.

6. Repeat this knot with each cord (D,E,F,G,H,I) until you have a complete row. To make the lines zig zag, bring cord B back across the cords I,H,G, F,E,D and pin it in place or hold it this time with your left hand. Starting with I, tie a knot just as you did before (remember: do not move cord B). Finish all the knots in this row, then bring B back to the right side again.

7. Zig zag the lines until you have made the piece long enough to fit around your neck or head. Loop the ends around a second ring and cut off the extra cord. Put a little glue on the ends, then press them against the cords as shown in the illustration at right. Let the glue dry completely, then tie the choker on your neck or head with a pretty ribbon threaded through the two rings.

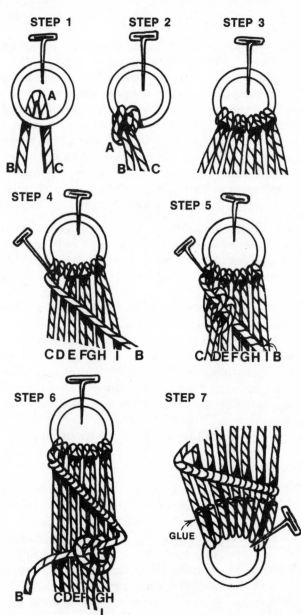

WITH TWINE AND A TWIST—A DOLL

Make a family of twine dolls, like the one shown here, for your doll house, as passengers for your toy cars, or as a decoration for the tree at Christmas time. The doll can be any size and made of jute, cotton seine, or rug yarn. After you have finished the doll you can add buttons for eyes and even make little clothes for it from scrap material.

1. First cut four cords (all the same color) each twenty-four inches long. Fold them in half, then hang them from the center over a pin on your working surface. Cut another cord about eight inches long. Fold one end of this extra cord and pin it next to the other cords on the board as shown below.

2. Take end A and begin wrapping it tightly around all the cords just above the end C. This is the neck of your doll so wrap just to the point where it would have a chin. Thread end A through loop B and remove pin from loop B (see illustration below). Then, firmly pull end C until you cannot see end A or loop B. Cut end C off below the doll's neck.

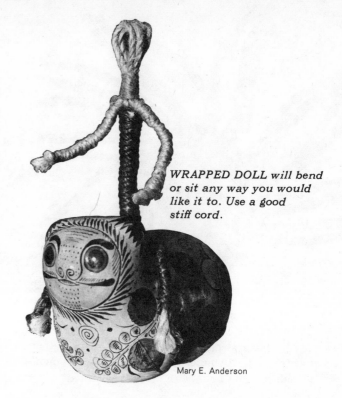

WRAPPED DOLL will bend or sit any way you would like it to. Use a good stiff cord.

Mary E. Anderson

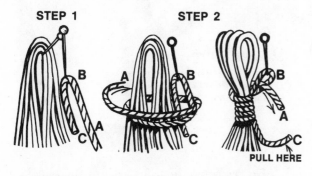

STEP 1   **STEP 2**

PULL HERE

3. Taking the two outside cords on both sides, you will now form the arms just like you did the neck. Cut two extra cords about ten inches long each, then fold the extra cords at one end. Place them on either side next to the two cords you will wrap. Start the wrapping at the point where you would like the doll's hands, then wrap the cord up to the neck (see illustration below). After you have pulled loop and wrapping end down into the arm, cut off extra cord leaving some ends for the doll's hands.

4. To wrap the body, take a different color cord (about twenty inches long) and start the wrapping around all six center cords just below the point of the doll's waist (see illustration below). Wrap up to the neck again.

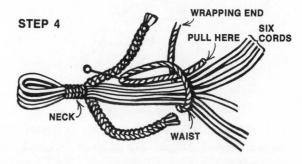

STEP 4

WRAPPING END

PULL HERE

SIX CORDS

NECK

WAIST

5. For its legs, take three cords on one side and three on the other side, then wrap from the doll's feet up to its waist.

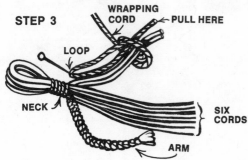

STEP 5

WRAPPING END

PULL HERE

THREE CORDS

LEG

6. Cut all the extra cord off. Now you can give the doll eyes, hair, or anything you would like to add.

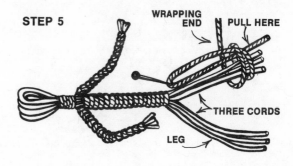

STEP 3

WRAPPING CORD — PULL HERE

LOOP

NECK

SIX CORDS

ARM

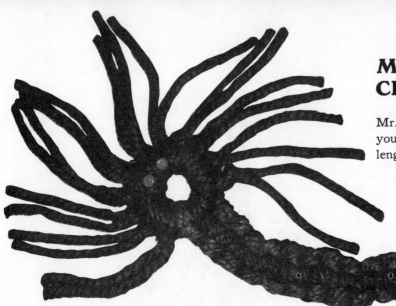

MR. SEYMOUR CENTIPEDE

Mr. Centipede can be a friendly companion when you play, work, or sleep. He can be any color, any length, or any size you would like him to be.

1. First find a wooden drapery ring; this will be his head. Cut eleven cords of heavy yarn, each twenty inches long. Fold one of the cords in half and put the loop (A) under the drapery ring as shown in the illustration below.

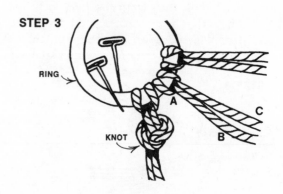

Oren Peterson Age: 8

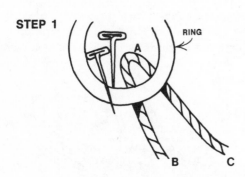

STEP 1

SQUARE KNOT is main knot used in Mr. Centipede's tail. He is made of soft rug yarn.

2. Pull the loop over the drapery ring and then thread the ends B and C through loop A and pull the ends so the knot is tight around the ring. (See illustration below.)

3. Do the same thing for each of the remaining ten cords; about ¾ of the drapery ring will be covered. Take the ends of each cord together and tie a knot right next to the drapery ring. This completes Seymour's head and gives him twenty-two legs. (See illustration below.)

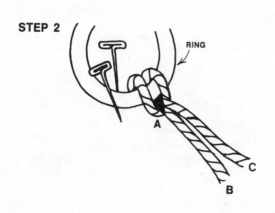

STEP 2

STEP 3

4. Next cut two cords of different colors each about 3⅓ yards long. Cut a third cord of the same color as Seymour's legs, about 2½ yards long. Fold the three cords in half and loop them onto the last ¼ of the drapery ring the same as you did his legs. Put the cord which is the same as the color of his legs in the center of the other two cords. This time do not knot them.

Have someone help you wind the four long outside cord ends into two bobbins of two cords each (see instructions on page 11). Pin Mr. Centipede to the working surface. Tape or pin the center cords BB to the board as shown below (these cords will never move while you are tying knots around them).

STEP 4

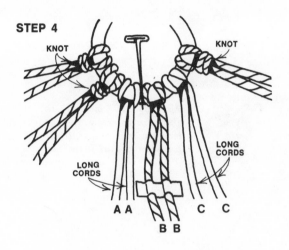

5. Take cords AA, place them over BB and under CC. You can hold cords BB instead of pinning or taping them, but hold them straight and tight while you move the other cords around them. (See illustration below.)

STEP 5

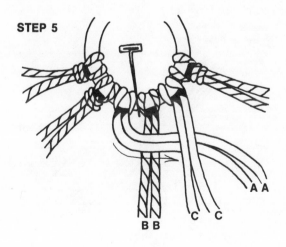

6. Take cords CC, place them under BB, pull them up behind AA and through the loop between AA and BB as shown below.

STEP 6

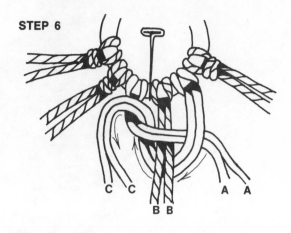

7. Take cord AA again and bring it back over BB and under CC. Pull cord CC under BB, then up through the loop between BB and AA. Pull the knot tight (see illustration).

STEP 7

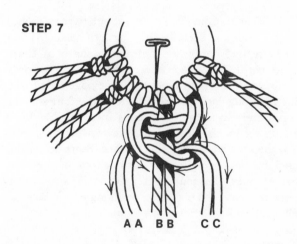

This is the first knot of Mr. Centipede's tail. Continue knotting down cords BB repeating the same steps as this first knot until Mr. Centipede is about twenty-five inches long. Tie a knot with each of the two outside cord ends AA and CC. Tie another knot with the cords BB. Trim Mr. Centipede's legs around his head and his tail with the scissors. Tie a few knots at intervals in the ends of his tail. Stick two colored tacks into the drapery ring to be his eyes. Now Mr. Centipede is ready to follow you anywhere.

A LEASH FOR YOUR PET

You may have the only pet on the block with such an unusual macramé leash. It is sturdy but simple to make. Find a metal hook to put on the end and some strong cord such as cotton seine twine, jute, or nylon.

PROUD DOG is ready to show off his new macramé leash made of spiraling half knots and jute cord.

Bryan DeVore Age: 7½

1. Measure four cords each about twenty inches longer than you need for the length of a leash. Then measure two cords five times the length of these other cords. Have each end of these two long cords wrapped into separate bobbins (see page 11). Place the two long cords on either side of the four shorter cords and tie all six cord ends into one big knot about six inches down from the top of the cords. Pin the knot to the working surface. Start below the knot by first bringing left cord A (one of the long cords) over the four center cords B and under outside right cord C (the second long cord). See the illustration below.

2. Bring right cord C under the B cords and up through the loop formed between A and B cords. This is knot number one; see the illustration below. This is called the half knot because it is the first part of the square knot. (If further instruction is necessary see page 22.)

STEP 1

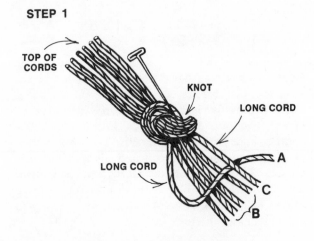

STEP 2

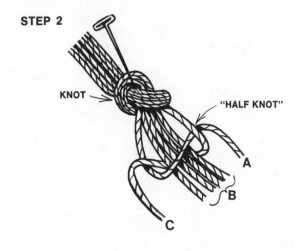

3. Starting from the left side again, bring cord C over the B cords and under A. Then pull A under B cords and up through the loop formed between B cords and C. (See illustration below.)

As you continue knotting, you will notice how the knots try to twist. Do not try to keep the cords flat. Just make sure you always start a knot with the cord nearest to the left side. If you do this your knots will twist with no problem.

STEP 3

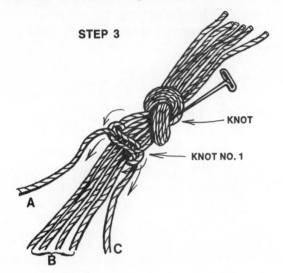

4. Once you have knotted about ten or twelve inches, make a loop with the twelve inches of knots to form a handle for your leash. Put the cord ends which were tied in the beginning big knot next to the cord ends you have not yet knotted. Untie the big knot and place the cord ends next to B cords. Continue your knotting with cords A and C, but use the B cords as well as these other cord ends in the center of your knots. This secures the loop of your handle (see illustration below).

STEP 4

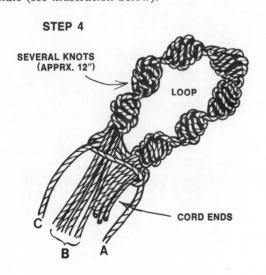

5. Keep knotting until the leash is just a little shorter than the length you would like. Pull all the B cords through the metal clip. Put a little dab of white glue on the ends and press them to the four B cords. Continue knotting about eight knots with ends A and C over all the glued ends. (See illustration below.)

STEP 5

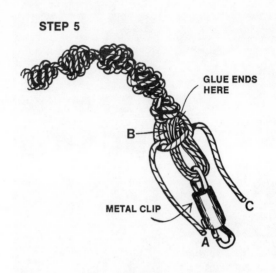

6. To make it even more secure, take an extra piece of cord twelve inches long and fold it at one end. Pin the folded end (2) next to the last knot you completed. Starting near the top of the metal clip, wind the other end of the extra cord (1) around and around tightly over all the cord ends A, cords B, and C never overlapping (see process for doll, page 61). When you reach the point of loop 2, thread end 1 through the loop. (See illustration below.)

Pull cord end 3 down until loop 2 and cord 1 disappear into the wrapping. Cut cord end 3 off. Now your leash is ready for your pet.

STEP 6

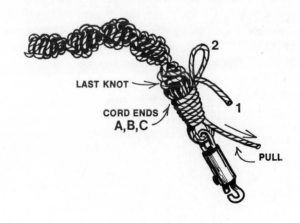

AN ELABORATE MACRAMÉ BELT

The macramé belt shown here is made of four different knots. It is a more advanced project, and one which will take much more time than the other projects in this chapter. But when you finish the belt, it will be the pride of your wardrobe.

Leslie Ann Forrester Age: 12

MACRAMÉ BELT is made from a soft rug yarn which is washable and easy to knot.

Cut twelve lengths of heavy yarn or cotton cord, each four times longer than the measurement of your waist plus twenty-five inches. Tie a knot in the ends of the cords and pin them next to each other on a working surface. Wrap the other ends into bobbins (explained on page 11).

1. On the left outside cord measure three inches down from the knot. At this point, pull cord A (holding cord) straight across all the other cords (B,C,D,E,F,G,H,I,J,K,L). Pin it at the point where it bends (see illustration below).

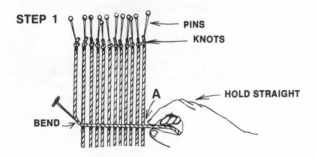

2. Holding cord A with one hand, loop cord B around and behind it always keeping A tight and straight across the other cords.

3. Again, loop cord B around and behind cord A, then pull cord B through the loop as shown in the illustration below. This is called a double half hitch (the same as shown on pages 15 and 60). Continue knotting with cords C through L until all of them have been looped twice around cord A. Then, put cord A down next to the last cord L.

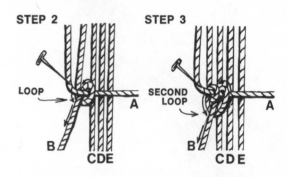

4. Divide all the cords into three groups of four cords each. With the first group (cords B,C,D,E), tie what iş called a square-knot chain (the same as shown on pages 25 and 62). To do this, bring cord B over on top of cords C and D then under cord E. (See illustration below.)

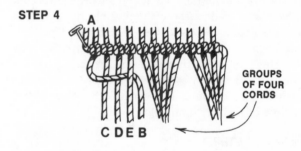

5. Pull cord E under cords C and D, then through the loop between cords B and C (see illustration).

6. Next bring cord B back across cords C and D then under cord E as shown in the illustration below.

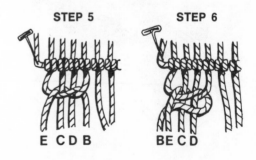

7. Finish the knot by pulling E under C and D, then up and out through the loop between B and D (see illustration). Pull the knot tight.

STEP 7

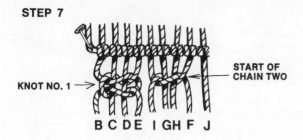

KNOT NO. 1 →

→ START OF CHAIN TWO

B C D E I G H F J

8. Repeat the steps above five times with the same cords. Cord B will always be on top and cord E will always be on the bottom as shown in the illustration below. Make two more square knot chains with the remaining groups (cords F,G,H,I and J,K,L,A). Make certain all three chains have the same number of knots.

STEP 8

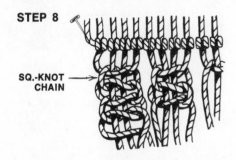

SQ.-KNOT CHAIN →

9. Pull cord A back straight across the bottom of the three chains; pin it at the bend and hold the other end with your hand. Starting with cord L, loop it twice just as you learned in the first row of knots (see illustration below). Loop each cord twice over cord A then place A down on the left side of B.

STEP 9

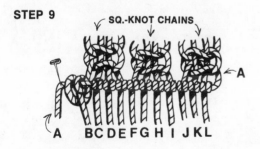

↓ SQ.-KNOT CHAINS ↓

← A

A   B C D E F G H I J K L

10. The next section of the belt is the alternate square-knot pattern (the same as shown on page 27). You will use the same knot as you did in the chain,

the square knot. Divide the cords into three groups of four cords. Knot one square knot with each group (see illustration below).

STEP 10

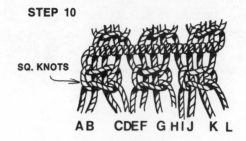

SQ. KNOTS →

A B   C D E F   G H I J   K L

11. Put aside the two outside cords on each side and divide the remaining center cords (C,D,E,F and G,H,I,J) into two groups. Knot a square knot with each group as shown below.

STEP 11

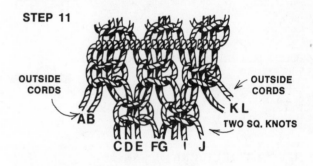

OUTSIDE CORDS →

← OUTSIDE CORDS

↘ AB

K L ↙

TWO SQ. KNOTS ←

C D E   F G   I   J

12. Bring the two outside cords back next to the other cords. Divide the cords into three equal groups of four cords. Knot a square knot with each group.

STEP 12

→ THREE SQ. KNOTS

TWO SQ. KNOTS →

→ THREE SQ. KNOTS

A B   C D E F   G H I   J K L

Now repeat the three sections you have just learned until you knot to the full length of your cords. The pattern is: one row of loops (double half hitches), three square knot chains, a row of loops (double half hitches), three rows of square knots (alternate square-knot pattern), and a row of loops (double half hitches). Finish your belt with a row of loops, then cut the cord ends into an even fringe, the same length as on the beginning end of the cords.

GLOSSARY

ALTERNATE SQUARE KNOTS (also called alternating square knots). Square knots tied in horizontal rows alternating so as to form a row of knots below and between the knots of the previous row. See page 27.

DOUBLE HALF HITCH (also called clove hitch). Two loops over a stationary cord or support. See page 15.

DOUBLE HALF HITCH BARS (also called cording). Several double half hitches tied in horizontal rows. See page 16.

HALF HITCH (also called buttonhole knot, tatting knot, simple knot, blanket stitch). A single loop over a stationary cord or support. See page 14.

HALF-HITCH CHAINS (also called sennits, see-saw knots). Half hitches or double half hitches tied vertically in succession. See page 20.

HALF KNOT (also called macramé knot). The first or last part of a square knot. See page 22.

HALF-KNOT CHAIN (also called half-knot sennit, spiral). Several half knots tied in succession vertically. See page 23.

JOSEPHINE KNOT (also called carrick bend, Chinese knot). A flat oval-shaped knot formed by cords woven over and under each other. See page 45.

MOUNTING KNOT (also called Lark's head, reverse Lark's head). A method of securing cords onto a cord or support from which a knotted piece is begun. See page 13.

ORIENTAL MATTING (also called Chinese matting). A form of Josephine knot using two loops and weaving the ends of each throughout the knot. See page 47.

OVERHAND KNOT (also called thumb knot, shell knot). A simple looped knot using one or more tying cords. See page 12.

PLAITING (also called braiding). A method of braiding cords to gather them into one unit. See page 48.

REVERSE DOUBLE HALF HITCH (also called Lark's head, mounting knot on its side). The mounting knot just tied vertically. See page 20.

SQUARE KNOT (also called flat knot, reef knot, Solomon's knot). Two or more cords tied over many cords or none. See page 24.

SQUARE-KNOT BOBBLE (also called ball, flat knot ball, button). A short square-knot chain pulled back over itself into a ball and secured with a final square knot. See page 26.

SQUARE-KNOT CHAIN (also called square-knot sennit, Solomon's bar, flats). Several square knots tied in succession vertically. See page 25.

TURK'S HEAD. A further developed knot stemming from Josephine knot but using one end to weave continuously over and under throughout the knot. See page 46.

VERTICAL DOUBLE HALF HITCH. A double half hitch using what is normally the tying cords as holding cords and the one holding cord as a tying cord. See page 21.

WRAPPING. A method of securing many cords into one unit by binding them with one cord. See page 44.